The Book of Revelation

"Time is Currency"

Albert Salazar

Printed in the United States of America

Published by:
D'Anointed Heart Book Publishing, LLC
CEO: Yneka Hathorn All rights reserved.
E: danointedheartpublishing@gmail.com
PO: 346.316.1109 PM: 346.757.2350

©September 2024
ISBN: 9798340375247

Unless otherwise noted all scripture is taken from the NKJV version of the bible.

Spring, TX

Cover designed and illustrated by Tasally Tarannum and Yneka Hathorn

Table of Contents

TIME IS CURRENCY

I heard a man say, that "Time is Currency, a Gift we can only spend once. It is more valuable than money, or the things we grasp for in this life."

James says it this way:
"For what is your life? It is even a vapor that appears for a little time and then vanishes away."
James 4:14

Eternity is endless, but time is measured by a "Beginning" and an "End."

"Time" from a Biblical perspective can be defined as a beginning with Creation in **(Genesis 1:1)** and an ending with the second coming of Christ, at which time the world order as we know it will be terminated."

(2 Peter 3:8-13)
Probably the best way to say it is that, "time" is a God placed Parenthesis, within the course of eternity.

We are each given a certain amount of this precious resource from God, an opportunity in which to encounter His redemptive work and make the greatest eternal decision we can ever make, our Salvation.

Carl F. H. Henry defined time as "the divinely created sphere of God's preserving and redemptive work, and the arena of man's decision on his way to an eternal destiny."

The Book of Revelation is about the ultimate consummation of God's divine purpose for this world. "Time" is quickly moving towards that goal, which will be realized at the time of Christ's return.

Paul confirms this in:
I Corinthians 15:24
"Then comes the end when he shall deliver up the kingdom to God....."

Time is a neutral and important element, it does nothing on its own, but it does provide humanity a God given opportunity for each of us to decide whether to receive God's precious gift of forgiveness through Christ or not.

Romans 13:11
"And do this, knowing the time, that now it is high time to awake out of sleep; for now our salvation is nearer than when we first believed."

The greatest revelation we can all experience in "Time" is realizing how much God loves us through His Son Jesus.

Don't waste the precious currency you've been given!

Let us open in prayer!

Father, bless our time of study. We pray that you open the eyes of our understanding in order for us to know the hope which you have provided us and that we may discover the riches of your glorious inheritance for your holy people. May we speak out of a heart filled with faith, may our words encourage, give hope, peace, joy, and may they point people to the Cross of Christ.

In Jesus name Amen!

Revelation 12:11:

Says that *"we will overcome our enemy by the blood of the lamb, and the word of our testimony. "*

Let me begin by saying, that we read and experience the Bible as a storyline of a play; the curtain rises up in Genesis and it comes down in the book of Revelation.

In between we find a kaleidoscope of stories, all charged with life- changing events and faith-filled people.
The Main Character is GOD, the Father/Son/Holy Spirit.
The Conflict: Sin.
The Theme: Humanities Redemption.

As we focus on the book of Revelation. It is an easy book to understand, if we have read the first 65 books of the Bible prior to it.

It stands to reason that, just as you couldn't pick up any other book, read the last chapter desiring to understand what the storyline was all about. This is also true with Revelation. This book gives us a prophetic view/picture of what God has prepared for the future of His children and the end of this world as we know it.

I want to lay out two general outlines that scripture provides beginning with:

Revelation 1:19
This verse is probably the most important one in the entire book, because it serves as our general outline. Jesus told John,
'*Write the things which you have seen, and the things which are and the things which will take place after this.*"

This is what Jesus is directing John to write: _the things which he had just seen_ – past tense (chapter one). Jesus reveals himself to John. In fact, that is what the word Apocalypse means to uncover/reveal. The fact is that in all John writes, he feels that his writing has the purpose of sharing what he has seen, heard, and handled.

According to 1 John, 1: 1–4
"That which was from the beginning, which we have heard, which we have seen with our eyes, which we have looked upon, and our hands have handled, concerning the word of life – the life was manifested, and we have seen, and bear witness, and declared to you that eternal life, which was with the Father, was manifested to us that which we have seen and heard, we declared to you, that you also may have fellowship with us; and truly our fellowship is with the father and with his son, Jesus Christ. And these things we write to you that your joy may be full"

What John saw, was Jesus revealed among the lamp-stands.

Jesus continues "_and with the things which are_" – present tense, (chapter 2–3) these would be the letters that Jesus dictates to John, one for each of the 7 churches.

Then Jesus concludes with the
"things which will take place after this."
The Greek words are (Meta Tauta)
(Chapters 4-22) future tense.

Jesus is referring to the things that will happen
after the "Rapture"
The second outline is the Biblical layout,
that we will follow in our Study, that I have
already laid out in the Table of Contents.

Our storyline begins with John on the Island of
Patmos.
Tradition tells us that the Roman Emperor
Domitian banished him to Patmos around AD
95.

Jesus Reveals Himself to John
Chapter 1

"The Revelation of Jesus Christ, which God gave Him to show His servants—things which must shortly take place. And He sent and signified it by His angel to His servant John, who bore witness to the word of God, and to the testimony of Jesus Christ, to all things that he saw. Blessed is he who reads and those who hear the words of this prophecy and keep those things which are written in it; for the time is near.

John, to the seven churches which are in Asia Grace to you and peace from Him who is and who was and who is to come, and from the seven Spirits who are before His throne, and from Jesus Christ, the faithful witness, the firstborn from the dead and the ruler over the kings of the earth. To Him who loved us and washed us from our sins in His own blood and has made us kings and priests to His God and Father, to Him be glory and dominion forever and ever. Amen.

Behold, He is coming with clouds, and every eye will see Him, even they who pierced Him. And all the tribes of the earth will mourn because of Him. Even so, Amen. "I am the Alpha and the Omega, the Beginning and the End," says the Lord, "who is and who was and who is to come, the Almighty."

John explains the Vision of the Son of Man that he saw.

Revelation 1:9-11

I, John, both your brother and companion in the tribulation and kingdom and patience of Jesus Christ, was on the island that is called Patmos for the word of God and for the testimony of Jesus Christ. I was in the Spirit on the Lord's Day, and I heard behind me a loud voice, as of a trumpet, saying, "I am the Alpha and the Omega, the First and the Last," and, "What you see, write in a book and send it to the seven churches which are in Asia: to Ephesus, to Smyrna, to Pergamos, to Thyatira, to Sardis, to Philadelphia, and to Laodicea."

John writes a word Picture of Jesus among the Lampstands;

V.12-20

"Then I turned to see the voice that spoke with me. And having turned I saw seven golden lampstands, and in the midst of the seven lampstands, One like the Son of Man, clothed with a garment down to the feet and girded about the chest with a golden band. His head and hair were white like wool, as white as snow, and His eyes like a flame of fire; His feet were like fine brass, as if refined in a furnace, and His voice as the sound of many waters; He had in

His right hand seven stars, out of His mouth went a sharp two-edged sword, and His countenance was like the sun shining in its strength. And when I saw Him, I fell at His feet as dead. But He laid His right hand on me, saying to me, "Do not be afraid; I am the First and the Last. I am He who lives, and was dead, and behold, I am alive forevermore. Amen. And I have the keys of Hades and of Death. Write the things which you have seen, and the things which are, and the things which will take place after this. The mystery of the seven stars which you saw in my right hand, and the seven golden lamp-stands:

Although John had been with Jesus for about three years, had heard Him speak to thousands, watched as He performed miracles and healed the sick. On many occasions he probably sat down to eat with Him. Yet John had never seen Jesus as He appeared to Him on that Island in that moment. Jesus has a way of doing that, just when you think you know Him and seem comfortable with that, He reveals another facet of Himself to us. May that happen to you as you read this text.

What was the meaning of all the objects surrounding Jesus, what did they represent?

The Book of Revelation is about Jesus being revealed to John and to every reader after him. Some have said that Revelation is a closed Book, not to be understood. But it is quite the opposite. As you can see just by the outlines I've already given you. It is the Unveiling of the Truth. It is a book that opens up the truth to all who take the time to read and study it. In fact, it promises blessings, *"Blessed is he who reads and those who hear the words of this prophecy and keep those things which are written in it;"*

All of the strange Imagery that is encountered in Revelation, have already been written about and explained in the 65 books prior to it.

<u>Note</u>: The Seven Stars (angels) represent the pastors of the seven churches, and the seven lamp-stands are the seven churches.

The question is: Why should we want to know about these seven churches?

The reasons are simple and understandable because:

1-These were real churches.

2-They also give us an overview of Church history.

3-Because they speak to us prophetically about the condition of the Church as time has progressed.

4-These letters paint a clear picture of where we are on God's timeline.

The condition of the church digressed as time went on, the disciples began with an apostolic church, and in the end we wind up with an Apostate church. It begins with a church that has lost its love for Christ and we end up with a totally corrupt church, that Jesus has nothing good to say about. In fact, He paints a picture of Himself being locked out and having to knock and ask to be allowed to come in.

Revelations, 3:20
"Behold I stand at the door and ask if anyone hear my voice and open the door, I will come into him and sup with him and him with me."

This verse is part of the letter that Jesus sends to the Church of Laodicea. He was trying to come in and help them change. But they would not allow Him.

Each of these letters speaks to us individually and collectively because of this, you will find yourself as part of one these churches.

In Chapter 4, We find John is now in heaven, safe and secure in God's presence.

He sees an Open Door in Heaven

Revelation 4:1-5 The Throne Room of Heaven.

"After these things I looked, and behold, a door standing open in heaven. And the first voice which I heard was like a trumpet speaking with me, saying, "Come up here, and I will show you things which must take place after this." At once I was in the Spirit, and behold, a throne stood in heaven, with one seated on the throne. And he who sat there had the appearance of jasper and carnelian, and around the throne was a rainbow that had the appearance of an emerald. Around the throne were twenty-fourth thrones, and seated on the thrones were twenty-four elders, clothed in white garments, with golden crowns on their heads. From the throne came flashes of lightning, and rumblings and peals of thunder, and before the throne were burning seven torches of fire, which are the seven spirits of God,"

We identify the "_seven spirits of God_" as the fullness of the Holy Spirit,

Why is the number seven used to describe him? Because this number is perfect and it refers to the Holy Spirits perfection and completion.

In Biblical terms 7 is considered a perfect and complete number.

-There are 7 Days of the week

-Seven notes in a musical scale

-Jesus taught Peter to forgive 70x7

-There are 7 Stars, 7 Thunders, 7 Bowl Judgements

Isaiah gives us greater insight into these 7 Spirits.

Isaiah 11:1

*"A shoot will come up from the stump of Jesse;
From his roots a Branch will bear fruit.
The Spirit of the LORD will rest on him—
the Spirit of wisdom and of understanding,
the Spirit of counsel and of might,
the Spirit of the knowledge and fear of the
LORD and he will delight in the fear of the
LORD."*

Those are the 7 aspects of completeness and wholeness in the Holy Spirit.

Now the #8 is considered a new beginning. Jesus is considered our new beginning because the eighth day was the first day after Creation.

I want to introduce the word, <u>Gematria</u>:
This was practice or a method of assigning a
numerical value to each letter of a word, name,
or expression to understand if there is any
hidden meaning in that word. The word
gematria is of Hebrew origin.
When you add all the Numerical Value of
the letters in Jesus, they total 888. The number
value of satan's name is 13. This number system
was used in olden days to interpret prophecies.

As we study these 7 letters, to the Churches,
I want you to examine your own life and
determine
*"Which of these letters would Jesus write and
send you in light of how you are living your life
in the current cultural and spiritual atmosphere,
we are in today?"*

1. Each Letter was written to a church that
                actually existed in that day.

2. Each letter was directed to the
        Angel/Pastor of that Congregation
        and he was expected to respond to them.

3. They were expected to respond positively
        or face the consequences.
4. Each letter is the same in respect
        to form but not in message.

There is a:
a. Commendation
b. Correction
c. Consequences.

The message was different for each one; Except, Smyrna and Philadelphia they did not get a Correction and Laodicea did not get a Commendation.

The reason for these letters: were to encourage each individual and congregation to do their best to examine themselves in light of the message Jesus was giving them. We know each of these letters came from Jesus because He takes the time to introduce himself.

He begins his introduction to John with a blessing:

Revelation 1:3
"Blessed is he who reads and those who hear the words of this prophecy and keep those things which are written in it; for the time is near."

Revelation 1:11
"saying, "I am the Alpha and the Omega, the First and the Last," and, "What you see, write in a book and send it to the seven churches which are in Asia: to Ephesus, to Smyrna, to

Pergamos, to Thyatira, to Sardis, to Philadelphia, and to Laodicea."

Revelation 1:19-20
"Write the things which you have seen, and the things which are, and the things which will take place after this."

The mystery of the seven stars which you saw in my right hand, and the seven golden lamp-stands:

"The seven stars are the angels of the seven churches, and the seven lamp-stands which you saw are the seven churches."

It is a blessing for me personally to realize, that as a Pastor, Jesus holds me in His right hand. Each element Jesus mentions, represents something or someone:

The stars were the pastors or bishops of the seven churches, symbolized by the lamp stands. A pastor is God's messenger to that church, and he is responsible to faithfully teach/preach God's word to them. The fact that they are held in his right hand is significant because He protects, upholds, and guides these leaders with His strength and wisdom.

The Lamp-stands represent the Churches, so as he stands in the midst of them, it means that every time we meet as the church, wherever we go Jesus is with us.

Angels is another word he uses to represent the Pastors.

Each Church - also represents the state of the church at different time periods in Church History.
But these letters also represent His message to the Church of today !
To you and I!

They communicate:
1. A Word of Commendation and Encouragement.
2. A Message of Correction.
3. And the Consequences, the final result if His message is not attended to. In the Midst of all the Sugar and Sweetness we hear today, of God's Love for us and while that is true and all good.

4. We must also understand that each of us have a Personal Responsibility. What will we do with what we know to be Truth!

Let us pray:

Lord open our understanding to your
Prophetic Word that we be filled with
your Wisdom, to know what we should do in
our generation as we walk in Your Spirit of
light and the fear of the LORD. That we be able
to examine ourselves, and be able see where
the Church is Individually and Collectively on
Your Timetable. And how we stand before
you Spiritually, individually. That we may all
be found faithful so that we can stand against
the power of evil in our life time. Holy Spirit
arise in each of us, Guide us as we study your
word.

His Love Letters to the Churches
Chapter 2-3

My wife owns a box of Love Letters written almost 85 years ago by a young soldier as he writes to his wife, while on the battlefields of Europe and North Africa. In them he expresses how much He loves and misses her and looks forward to seeing her again soon, that soldier was my Father in Law.

As we read Jesus' Love Letters, to the 7 Churches in Asia. We can sense the Love and Concern that he had for them as he prepares to present them all to His Father. Let us begin with the first letter to the loveless church, Ephesus.

Revelation 2:1-7
"To the angel of the church of Ephesus write, 'These things says He who holds the seven stars in His right hand, who walks in the midst of the seven golden lampstands:"

The 7 stars are the Pastors/Messengers of each church. Jesus walks in the midst of the seven golden lamp-stands that represent the Congregations.

Jesus begins by introducing Himself to John, as the author of these letters.
The word Angel/Messenger here, is used more as a Title rather than the identity of a being.
Jesus addresses the letter to the Pastor or Overseer of the Congregation.

In the Old Testament when Jesus would appear, in His Pre-incarnate state. He was referred to, as the Angel of the Lord.
Here, Jesus begins with His commendation for the church.

V.2-3
"I know your works, your labor, your patience, and that you cannot bear those who are evil. And you have tested those who say they are apostles and are not and have found them liars; and you have persevered and have patience and have labored for My name's sake and have not become weary."

As we examine these verses further. Jesus begins by saying, *"I know your works, labor, and patience"*
These are great traits for a Church to have! But we must understand that our works do not make us righteous, nor do they save us!
But it is also true of every individual who is truly saved, that Salvation brings about an

active faith that produces good works. So when the Lord *"declares that He knows their labor and patience."*

Although this Church had done many good things, they had persevered through many hardships and trials, hated evil, would not Compromise, or tolerate those who were evil. This is a weaknesses in the Church TODAY! Many have allowed evil into the body, they have compromised and allowed ungodly, unscriptural lifestyles and practices to enter into the Church.

(What I'm saying is that everyone should be allowed to attend a church service! But these Churches have allowed people who practice ungodly lifestyles to become leadership within the body without requiring change from them.)

Eph. 4:20-23
"But you have not so learned Christ, if indeed you have heard Him and have been taught by Him, as the truth is in Jesus: that you put off, concerning your former conduct, the old man which grows corrupt according to the deceitful lusts, and be renewed in the spirit of your mind, and that you put on the new man which was

created according to God, in true righteousness and holiness."

The Pope made an announcement in Dec. 2023 that priests could now begin to bless same sex couples. This is just one step closer to accepting same sex marriages.

The Church is under extreme pressure today to accept the rights of people who live an evil lifestyle and accept things as true when they are not. Things Like: (transgenders, cross dressers and homosexuals).
All under the guise of Love. This is totally contrary to the love that Jesus expresses in these letters.

And that same segment of people along with our government have actually tried to silence us from saying anything contrary to these destructive lifestyles.

The Church in Ephesus was not a compromising church, but as time moved on into church history, we find that the church began to compromise.

Ephesus was also a discerning congregation that tested those who said, they were apostles, when they were not. Making sure that these individuals were legitimate!

You see an apostle would have been a person who had walked with Jesus.

They also dealt with false teachers. Although this church remained steady, through the hard times; God looks beyond our outward appearance, activities and He looks into our hearts.

We must remember that John had actually walked with Jesus, and it appears as if there were false teachers who had come through, boasting that they too had been with Jesus during His earthly ministry, not realizing that John would have known that they were lying.

From what we have read, Ephesus was a well-organized and functioning Congregation.

As we look at all their works, labor and influence in the community, we could say that this was a great church. But even with all that,

The Lord said this to them:

In His correction, *v4*.

"Nevertheless I have this against you, that you have left your first love. Remember therefore from where you have fallen; repent and do the first works."

Although they had all of the motions of a great church they lacked the emotions of a great church.

In *1 Cor. 13:3,* Paul explains that a person can have so many gifted abilities, be actively involved in so many ministries in the church but if that individual doesn't have love, they are spiritually bankrupt.

All their actions are meaningless and will result in no rewards from God.

Love is the one characteristic that defines the church more than anything else. There is nothing greater than love. Because the Gospel is love and commands us to love Him and each other with all that we are. So whatever we do for God, must be motivated by love.

Paul wrote about the believers in Rome who were motivated by jealousies and envy, but this didn't trouble him because through it all Jesus was being preached. But when we all stand before Jesus our works will be examined by what manner they were. In other words what was our motivation when we did our works?

When people see us doing what we do in God's Kingdom; we may look very good and exemplary, but when we observe our hearts we may find that our motivation was all wrong we may be doing it to be acknowledged and praised by others.

Jesus said in the Sermon on the Mount,
Matthew 6:1
"Take heed that you do not do your charitable deeds before men, to be seen by them. Otherwise you have no reward from your Father in heaven."

The religious in Jesus' day, Prayed, Fasted, and Gave so others would judge them as being Spiritual. We must not allow our motive to be to impress others with our spirituality or knowledge.

Jesus culminates by saying, that if that is our motive? Then we already have our reward, we shouldn't expect anything more from God. You are wrong when you do anything that draws attention and praise to yourself.

Jesus also said,
Matthew 5:16
'Let your light so shine before men, that they may see your good works and glorify your Father in heaven." The Glory and Praise must be His, and His alone !

One day our works will be judged, whether they are motivated by Love, because these works are the only ones that God will accept. All I do must be considered a privilege and not a burden, all I do must be done because I love Him. I must understand, -I don't have too - I get too – And - I want too.

So we are encouraged in
Colossians 3:17
"And whatever you do in word or deed, do all in the name of the Lord Jesus, giving thanks to God the Father through Him."

In the Christmas Movie "It's a Wonderful Life" George Bailey had a difficult time with the responsibility he had in life, and it pushed him to his limit that he contemplated ending his life.

It is very easy to allow the oil in our lamps to run low/or out while fulfilling our responsibilities and just do things out of _rote_. _Definition_, (to do something mechanically or out of habit, repetitive or out of what we have learned.)

So that Serving God becomes something we do without passion it becomes dry and dead, without feelings of emotion.

Remember the ten virgins, five had oil to last them the night as they waited for the Bride Groom, yet five, of them were not diligent and ran out. We must not just do the busy work and neglect our interpersonal relationship with Him, because then we will be headed towards a situation we won't be able to answer.

The problem in Ephesus was that all they were doing was not being motivated by love. He tells them that this would be their consequence, (the good and the bad) If they choose NOT to change, "or else I will come to you quickly and remove your lamp-stand from its place—unless you repent."

Jesus Commendation to this church.
V. 6-7
"But this you have, that you hate the deeds of the Nicolaitans, which I also hate. "He who has an ear, let him hear what the Spirit says to the churches. To him who overcomes I will give to eat from the tree of life, which is in the midst of the Paradise of God."

Who were the Nicolaitans ?
If we look at the etymology of the word, Nicolaitans, it is derived from two Greek words.

Etymology is the study of the Origen of words:

1. _Nicos_ is the Greek word, from which Nike comes from, which means to conquer or subdue, victor or victory. This word is used in describing the church leadership.
2. The second word means _laity_. Nicolaitanism, therefore it is defined as the elevating of the clergy over the laity, which in the New Testament is heresy.

Jesus has become our high priest Our only Intermediary. Anything or anyone that gets between you and the Father, other than Jesus, "Is Heresy." Jesus is our only Mediator, not a man.

So He impresses upon them.

Revelation 2:5
"Remember therefore from where you have fallen; repent and do the first works, or else I will come to you quickly and remove your lampstand from its place—Unless you repent."

This scripture has three R's:
1. _Remember_- It is important to understand what Jesus is saying here, _'Take heed from where you have fallen,"_ Some people say I have

just lost my Love, No you didn't, _You walked away from it!_

What you need to do is come back to where you once were to the
A. Hot tears,
B. Deep passion
C. Desire you once had for God's Word, wanting to be in His presence, and to serve Him.

2. _Repent_, True Repentance, is accompanied by Sorrow, but sorrow alone is not enough. Many who do a crime feel sorrow but not because of what they did, but because they got caught doing it, True repentance brings Godliness.
3. _Repeat_ - Do what you did at the beginning!

So we must, _Remember_, _Repent and Repent_

Understand that with true repentance, change is eminent!

Many people do what they do for God out of a sense of:
A. Duty
B. Obligation
C. Responsibility
D. Or out of a sense of Earning their Salvation,

and because of this, never change.

Let us pray,
Lord, we repent and are willing to return to our first love, because at one time or another we have all been guilty of doing Kingdom work, out of a sense of duty, obligation, responsibility or out of a sense of earning our Salvation. We repent and are willingly return to our First Love.
Your Son our Savior and Mediator,
Jesus. Amen!

Now we come to the Church in Smyrna: Second letter. The Letter was written to the Persecuted Church.

As we study this letter we enter into the time period when the Church suffered the greatest persecution. From the moment of its birth until about the 315-316 AD., when Constantine passed the Edict of Toleration stopping the terrible persecution that the church had experienced for about 300 years.

In the beginning, the persecution came from the Jews, later it continued and got worse under the Romans, because Christian's would not worship their Emperor. When Constantine passed the Edict of Milan it granted Christianity the status of "religion licita," a form of worship that was recognized and accepted by the Roman Empire. It was the first edict legalizing Christianity.

The Greek word translated 'Smyrna' was used in the Septuagint (Greek Bible) to translate the Hebrew word for myrrh. This was a resin used as a perfume both for the Living,

— *Matt.* 2:11 as well as for the Dead — *John 19: 39.*

There are two similarities between the resin and this church. Both were associated with death and just as myrrh was produced by the crushing of the plant. So too, this church would be crushed by persecution, but in the process, give off its fragrant aroma through her faithfulness to God.

Revelation 2: 8-11

"And to the angel of the church in Smyrna write, 'these things says the First and the Last, who was dead, and came to life: "I know your works, tribulation, and poverty (but you are rich); and I know the blasphemy of those who say they are Jews and are not but are a synagogue of Satan. Do not fear any of those things which you are about to suffer. Indeed, the devil is about to throw some of you into prison, that

you may be tested, and you will have tribulation ten days. Be faithful until death, and I will give you the crown of life. "He who has an ear, let him hear what the Spirit says to the churches. He who overcomes shall not be hurt by the second death."

Jesus begins by introducing himself as the Alpha and Omega these are the first and last letters of the Greek Alphabet and all that is in between. There was no one before Jesus and there will be no one after Him.

Because Smyrna would have to confront death for their faith, Jesus continues by mentioning that He had been dead but now was alive. Letting them know that He is the hope of their resurrection. He says, *"I know your works, tribulation, and poverty"*

The majority of these church members were poor. If a rich person became a Christian the Roman Government would confiscate all they owned. Jesus mentions their lack of material possessions, He said, you may not have many material possessions but spiritually you are very rich.

Let me say this, we will never get a true measure of our wealth by what our bank account says. The true measure of our treasure is in Heaven.

What we have laid up for eternity. When we die, we will leave every material thing here.

It will be what we laid up in Heaven that will last through-out eternity.

Some individuals who were rich on Earth will be poor in Heaven, and many who were poor on earth will be rich in Heaven.

Mathew 6: 19-21
"Don't lay up for yourselves treasures on earth, where moth and rust destroy and where thieves break in and steal; but lay up for yourselves treasures in heaven, where neither moth nor rust destroys and where thieves do not break in and steal. For where your treasure is, there your heart will be also."

Then Jesus mentions the Synagogue of satan, these were a group of unbelieving Jews who persecuted Christians. They were guilty of slandering the church in Smyrna and opposing the church in Philadelphia. According to historian Justin Martyr, the church in Smyrna was accused of cannibalism because they spoke of eating the flesh and drinking the blood of Jesus.

At first, the majority of the persecution in the New Testament church faced came from the Jewish community.

The turning point for Christianity in the Roman Empire came in the form of a vision God gave Constantine, nearly three hundred years after the death of Jesus. The Lord mentions ten days of suffering, He could have been referring to the 10 emperors that would reign over Rome from Caesar to Diocletian. Yet believers have always suffered some form of persecution or another throughout church history. Although we may not see it here in the United States, It has existed and even now exists, across the world in different nations.

According to the latest _World Watch-list Report_ on Christian persecution:

1-There are 13 Christians worldwide killed every day because of their faith.
2-Everyday 12 churches or Christian buildings are attacked.
3-Every day, 12 Christians are unjustly arrested or imprisoned, and another five are abducted.

These are the reports of the 2021 world watch list. These numbers are probably more by now.

We must take notice that Smyrna is the only church that Jesus did not have any words of correction to give them. It appears as if though, it is in these extreme negative conditions that believers rise to meet the challenge.

While we were in China, I had the privilege to meet a Chinese Pastor who had been imprisoned by Mao Tse-tung the Communist leader of China in 1945. This Pastor spent the next 25 years in prison. When he was incarcerated his daughter was a baby, when he returned she was now a grown woman. We had the privilege of meeting them both. Yet through it all, these believers remained faithful to God and to their call. When he returned he was reinstated as the Pastor of that same church, he was now almost 90 years old.
To the Church in Smyrna Jesus says,
"To be faithful until death" this was not only meant to be Spiritual but to be fulfilled literally.
So amazing was the grace demonstrated by these believers filled with such peace and grace as they faced martyrdom that many actually welcomed it.

In doing so they emphasized the value and glory of living as well as dying for Christ.

The story of Poly Carp.....
I share with you his story, He was martyred in Smyrna around A.D. 155.
He had been the Bishop of that church. When he was about to be put to death, they were going to tie Him to the stake, but he assured his persecutors that it was not necessary, for he would not run. When the fire was lit, it circled around him but would not burn him. He did not die until a soldier was sent to pierce him with a weapon.

When asked to deny Christ and be allowed to live, this is how he answered, *"Eighty and six years I have served Him, and He has done me no wrong. How, then, could I blaspheme my King who saved me?....I bless Thee for (finding) deigning me worthy of this day and this hour that I may be among the martyrs and drink the cup of my Lord Jesus Christ.."*

There is an old hymn that says:
"May those who come behind us find us faithful"

Let us all strive to fulfill those words.

We have studied the:
1-Loveless Church
2-Persecuted Church

Now we arrive at the 3rd letter written to
Pergamum:
The Compromising Church.

Compromise begins when a person leaves their
first love for Jesus Christ, which in turn leads
to Compromise, then ultimately to Immorality,
Idolatry, and other Sins. When we begin to
compromise even a little, sin will eventually
enter into our lives.

We must understand that the moment
we become covenant makers with
wickedness, we become covenant breakers
with holiness. It's impossible to remain in a
covenant relationship with both.

James 4:4,
*"Do you not know that friendship with the world
is enmity with God?"*

This Church period is marked by the rise of
the office of the religious order we know today
as the office of the Pope.

When Constantine signed the Edict of Milan, in 313 AD, It was aimed to end the persecution of Christians, while the Edict of Thessalonica made Christianity the state religion of the Roman Empire.

The church was used to having external attacks of persecution but now satan, prepared a new strategy a different approach, He would attack them from within. Constantine's victory at "Milvian Bridge" under the Symbol of the Cross seemed to be a victory for the church.

With this victory:
1. He took sole control of the Western Empire of Rome. He assumed the title of Pontifex Maximus (Supreme High Priest)
2. Made Christianity the state religion.

This title would later be given to the bishop of Rome, as the Pope.

It was never God's intent for church and state to join together. Because if those leading the Church are wicked and politically ambitious individuals they will use the Church to get their way.

Revelation 2:12-17

*"And to the angel of the church in Pergamos
write, 'These things says He who has the sharp
two-edged sword: "I know your works, and
where you dwell, where satan's throne is. And
you hold fast to My name and did not deny my
faith even in the days in which Antipas was My
faithful martyr, who was killed among you,
where satan dwells. But I have a few things
against you because you have their those who
hold the Doctrine of Balaam, who taught Balak
to put a stumbling block before the children of
Israel, to eat things sacrificed to idols, and
to commit sexual immorality. Thus you also
have those who hold the Doctrine of the
Nicolaitans, which thing I hate. Repent, or else I
will come to you quickly and will fight against
them with the sword of My mouth. He who has
an ear, let him hear what the Spirit says to the
churches.
To him who overcomes I will give some of
the hidden manna to eat. And I will give him
a white stone, and on the stone a new
name written which no one knows except him
who receives it."*

This letter is one of encouragement, hope, and
correction to those in this church. It is also
a challenge for them, to return to the
exclusivity of Christ.

The fact is that God does not share His worship, nor does He allow compromise in the lives of those who believe in him. There is no compromise in God; so as his believers we shouldn't water down our beliefs, to accept things that are aren't right or real. Now, when we decide to stand on our convictions, rather than bow to the culture of the day, there will be those who will become upset about it because we won't validate or choose their opinion, decisions, lifestyle, or philosophy, over God's word. I believe that there is a lot of relevance between the day we are living in, and the church in Pergamum. This church was not persecuted for worshiping Jesus, they were oppressed because of their exclusive dedication to Him alone.

Let us look at what it would have been like to be a believer and live in Pergamum in that day.:

Jesus described it as satan's throne, because it was the place of worship for many of the Greek and Roman gods. Whatever people needed or wanted. The culture of the day offered them spiritual food from a variety of gods. There was a temple to Zeus, the Greek god over all other gods. He was the god of thunder and lightning and would use it against his enemies.

He was the god of power, if you needed something done, it was his temple that you would go to. But on the other hand if you wanted to party and celebrate, you could go to the Temple of Dionysius, the god of wine and revelry. Going to his temple would be like going to celebrate Mardi Gras. If you needed a good harvest you would go to the Temple of Demeter she could guarantee you food on your table. If you were sick you, you could go to the Temple of Asclepius, the god of healing. When the doctor couldn't find a cure for you, he would send his patients there. They would induce a sleep on the patient and then allow snakes to crawl over them, while they slept to bring about healing. In fact, our modern day symbol for medicine is two snakes coiled around a rod, and that symbol dates back to that time. Maybe you needed direction in life then you could go to the Temple of Athena, the goddess of wisdom. Or, maybe you wanted to honor Caesar for all the good that the Romans had given you, then you could go to the Roman temple.

That is why Jesus called Pergamum the place of satan's throne.

In our day: A church Pastor must continuously watch out for so many things and be careful about what is taught among the congregation. Today, people have access to so much information, some of it true and some not. And often times people try to bring wrong information and actions that are inconsistent to what the Bible teaches, that is what was happening in this church.

In that day, There were people who were advocating the Doctrine of Balaam. This doctrine began in the book of Numbers 22. When Balaam was unsuccessful at placing a curse on Israel, he instead devised a plan of seduction against them, causing Israel to commit spiritual and sexual immorality. The Hebrew men went after the Pergamum women.

The doctrine of Balaam is so serious and devious, because when satan's frontal attack doesn't work he will use the back door to attack. When he could not curse Israel, Balaam told King Balak how to get the Israelites to commit sin by enticing them to have sexual relations with foreign women and worship idols. The Israelites fell into these traps and God unleashed a deadly plague upon them as a result.

Numbers 31:16

"They were the ones who followed Balaam's advice and enticed the Israelites to be unfaithful to the LORD in the Beor incident, so that a plague struck the LORD's people."

What a tragedy! Balaam was willing to use his God given Office, abilities and talents for illicit gain. Our abilities and influence as spiritual leaders must never be up for sale. Peter writes about this type of people as he warns about us listening to deceptive false teachers.

2 Peter 2: 12-16
"But these, like natural brute beasts made to be caught and destroyed, speak evil of the things they do not understand, and will utterly perish in their own corruption, and will receive the wages of unrighteousness, as those who count it pleasure to carouse in the daytime. They are spots and blemishes, carousing in their own deceptions while they feast with you, having eyes full of adultery and that cannot cease from sin, enticing unstable souls. They have a heart trained in covetous practices and are accursed children. They have forsaken the right way and gone astray, following the way of Balaam the son of Beor, who loved the wages of unrighteousness; but he was rebuked for his

iniquity: a dumb donkey speaking with a man's voice restrained the madness of the prophet. These are wells without water, clouds carried by a tempest, for whom is reserved the blackness of darkness forever."

As I have already mentioned,
The Doctrine of the Nicolaitans: we must remember what this teaching is all about! If we look at the Etymology of the word, Nicolaitans, is derived from two Greek words. Nicos is the Greek word, from which Nike comes from, which means victor or victory this was used for the clergy.

The second word means laity. Nicolaitanism, therefore, is defined as elevating the clergy over the laity, which in the New Testament is heresy.
 Jesus at the cross became our High Priest our Intermediary. Anything or anyone that gets between you and the Father other than Jesus is heresy. Jesus is our only Mediator, not man. No man can forgive our sins but Christ. Like all false teachers, they abuse the Doctrine of Grace.

The church embraced this doctrine, filled with a licentious lifestyle and unrestrained, lawlessness. It seems that the "doctrine" of the

Nicolaitans taught that it was all right to have one foot in both worlds and that you didn't need be so strict about separating from the world in order to be a Christian.

Application: There is so much of this doctrine in the Church today.

Conclusion,
Jesus closes this letter with two promises:
"To him who overcomes I will give some of the hidden manna to eat. And I will give him a white stone, and on the stone a new name written which no one knows except him who receives it."

Now some people may already be paying a price for their faith: Maybe they're lonely because they keep looking for that right someone who loves Jesus, to fall in love with. Remember: "Be patient love will find you"

Maybe, people at work talk about you because you don't join in their sin filled activities and conversations. Maybe your spouse is not a believer and when you seek that spiritual support, it's not there. Maybe you don't have many friends, because you don't party and get involved sexually just to have a good time.

Jesus promises to give each overcomer:
1. The hidden manna to eat. This was the food God gave Israel that kept them alive as they journeyed through the desert. When we stop to think what that manna would look like for us today, think of the manna of His Presence, in those difficult moment. The sustaining power of His Word that comforts us. The presence and power of His Holy Spirit to strengthen you. The manna of revelation into His Word.

2. A white stone, and on it a name. Not much is known about this, but could it be, that Jesus was referring to the custom of that day. When someone of great stature was celebrating a party, an invitation would be sent out for that celebration with the name of the invitee on a marble stone with their name (Onoma) on it.

Could it be that Jesus was referring to His invitation, the celebration that He has prepared for each of us at the wedding supper of the Lamb, as we will receive our own private invitation to that great celebration with Him. This white stone could also mean this: When a person was convicted of a crime they were given either a white stone, indicating that

they would live, or be given a black stone, indicating that they would die.
Let us thank God for our white stone promise!

Revelation 19:9
"Then he said to me, "Write: Blessed are those who are called to the marriage supper of the Lamb!' "

We have arrived at the fourth Letter to the Corrupt Church -*Thyatira*
Revelation 2:18-29
"And to the angel of the church in Thyatira write, 'These things says the Son of God, who has eyes like a flame of fire, and His feet like fine brass: "I know your works, love, service, faith, and your patience; and as for your works, the last are more than the first. Nevertheless I have a few things against you, because you allow that woman Jezebel, who calls herself a prophetess, to teach and seduce My servants to commit sexual immorality and eat things sacrificed to idols. And I gave her time to repent of her sexual immorality, and she did not repent.
Indeed I will cast her into a sickbed, and those who commit adultery with her in great tribulation, unless they repent of their deeds.
I will kill her children with death, and all the churches shall know that I am He who searches

the minds and hearts. And I will give to each one of you according to your works. "Now to you I say, and to the rest in Thyatira, as many as do not have this doctrine, who have not known the depths of satan, as they say, I will put on you no other burden. But hold fast what you have till I come. And he who overcomes, and keeps My works until the end, to him I will give power over the nations—He shall rule them with a rod of iron; They shall be dashed to pieces like the potter's vessels'—as I also have received from My Father; and I will give him the morning star. "He who has an ear, let him hear what the Spirit says to the churches."

Jesus begins this letter with His personal introduction: as the "Son of God"
"And to the angel of the church in Thyatira write, These things says the Son of God: -Who has eyes like a flame of fire –"

He begins by emphasizing the fact that His eyes are able to penetrate and judge any situation. *"His feet are like fine burnished brass."* These words represent His purity and ability to be strong and unmovable.

In each letter Jesus uses terms that may not mean much to us today unless we take the time to study and understand the

circumstances in which these believers
were living in.

The fact that He uses words like burnished
brass to describe Himself. Bronze and
Brass are alloys that begin with the same basic
metal copper.
One is mixed with zinc and the other with
tin, these were the hardest metals of the day,
used to make tools or weapons. So they knew
what burnished brass looked like and what it
was capable of.

What would it have been like to live in Thyatira
in that day?

It was a wealthy town on the Lycus river:
1-It was filled with trade guilds, (Unions of
today) that manufactured textiles, bronze and
brass.
2. It was the center of the production of
a purple cloth, worn only by the rich
powerful and the high ranking military.
(Remember Lydia in the New Testament)

Every trade had a guild or a union. Yet, they
were more than just trade unions, these guilds
were tied into their business, social life and
religious worship. All uniquely joined together
into their entire lifestyle. When these guilds
would celebrate their reunions, they would do

so at the temples, dedicated to their gods. If believers did not attend, that would present a problem not only for them, but for the guild also.

The gods may not be pleased with their actions. Or if a Christian were asked to sculpt an idol god, and refused, they would be cancelled be _cancelled_ by the culture of the day. Serving God would hit them in their livelihood. (We have seen this happening to Christian's today).

But it appears that these believers had a more serious problem within themselves, there was deep corruption within the church.

Corruption is the dishonest/unscrupulous conduct of power by leadership.

Jesus continued His letter with His commendation:

Chap 2: 18
"I know your works, the last are more than the first. Your love, service, faith and patient endurance."

This church was on an upward trajectory, doing all these good things and doing more than at first.

But God wanted to remove the corruption:
v20.
"I have a few things against you have allowed that woman Jezebel who calls herself prophetess to teach and seduce my servants to teach and seduce my servants to commit sexual immorality and eat things sacrificed to idols."
(Remember that by doing this, they were paying homage or allegiance to these gods.)

Who was this woman Jezebel? How could the Pastor allow this false prophetess to teach this type of doctrine? (Some theologians believe that she could have been the Pastor's wife), Corruption ran deep in this church!

Revelation 2: 23
Jesus calls this woman and the church to repentance.
"I gave her time to repent, and she did not. I will cast her into a sickbed, And those who commit adultery with her and I will kill her children with death."

Our today application, We've been inundated with the fact that God loves us so much and while that is all true! This has caused many believers to find it difficult to understand that God is also just, He loves us, but He hates sin.

We would all like to think that this type of doctrine wouldn't be taught in the church today. But reality is that the corrupt culture of our day, is knocking at the door of every Christian church seeking validation for the sexually immoral lifestyles people live. On Dec. 19, 2023, the news reported that The Catholic Pope announced that it is alright to pray blessings over same sex couples because God loves them too. I am not advocating that we should not pray or love them, but our prayer should be that they repent and have a change of lifestyle.

Today when many churches are asked for their position on immoral lifestyles, any choose to say nothing. This is how and why these issues arise and remain in the church because many Pastors say nothing,

Then Jesus gives the results of His judgment:
Revelation 2 : 23
"and the churches shall know that I am he who searches the minds and hearts, and I will give to each one of you according to your works."

In all of this, Jesus takes time to express His appreciation and reminds the faithful.

Revelation 2: 24

"To those that don't have this doctrine, who have not known the depths of satan" Hold fast to what you have and keep my works"

What was this Doctrine?
(It was esoteric information, most secret societies deal in this, it is knowledge that only a few people are supposed to know, have or receive through sworn secrecy. Secret societies exist today on esoteric information !) But the point I want to make is that this passage gives us all hope, that even in the midst of the worst corruption , there was a group then that had not fallen prey to this woman. (Corruption)
In every period of history, when evil has been prevalent, there has always been a remnant of believers who have stood to oppose evil, resist the Devil, and chose to honor the Lord. (Noah was such a remnant when the whole human race was thoroughly evil *(Genesis 6:5)*.

What are the depths of satan that Jesus speaks of here? This teaching was secretive and profound, but it comes from satan and this woman had ensnared many undiscerning members of the church.

Jesus promises rewards to the over-comers.
Revelation 2: 26-28
"I will give him power to rule over the nations, to reign and rule with me."
I will give him the morning star –

(What Jesus is saying, is that He will give himself to that person)

Eschatology, is the study of the end time. It teaches us that at the moment of the rapture, every believer who is alive or dead will be taken up into heaven. And will remain there for about seven years while the tribulation is happening on earth. We will celebrate the Marriage Supper of the Lamb and the Judgment Seat of Christ during this time. Once the Tribulation is over, Christ will return to defeat the armies of the world that will be formed against Him; we will return with Him and after this last battle is over, the Bible says that all Christians are going to reign and rule with Him.

Revelation 20:4
"And they lived and reigned with Christ for a thousand years"
We will reign and rule with Him throughout the world.

What will we do in Christ's government?

We don't really know all of that! God wants to have some surprises for us. But, there is a connection between our faithfulness here on earth now, and whatever responsibility we are going to be given at that time. It is like the parable of the talents in **_Matthew 25:14-30_**. Jesus will reward us with responsibilities then, based on our faithfulness to Him, now. So Jesus' letter to Thyatira, is in reality His invitation to every believer of every generation, to remain faithful to His word; and they will reign and rule with Him.

Remember there is a small white stone prepared that represents your invitation to the Wedding Supper of the Lamb with your "Onoma" written on it. A white stone with the name of the invitee would be given when a great celebration would be had. Only those with the stone could come into celebrate.

We have arrived at the 5th Letter to Sardis
Revelation 3:1-6
"And to the angel of the church in Sardis write, 'These things says He who has the seven Spirits of God and the seven stars: "I know your works, that you have a name that you are alive, but you are dead. Be watchful, and strengthen the things which remain, that are ready to die, for I have not found your works

*perfect before God. Remember therefore how
you have received and heard; hold fast and
repent. Therefore if you will not watch, I will
come upon you as a thief, and you will not know
what hour I will come upon you. You have a few
names even in Sardis who have not defiled their
garments; and they shall walk with me in White,
for they are worthy.*
*He who overcomes shall be clothed in white
garments, and I will not blot out his name from
the Book of Life; but I will confess his name
before My Father and before His angels. "He
who has an ear, let him hear what the Spirit says
to the churches."*

When corruption exists in an organization, it
runs "deep." That is so true! If you all
remember the Enron Corp. The false returns
that they promised, and who can forget The
Bernie Madoff - Ponzi Scheme.

I want us all to notice that up to now, each
letter has been written to meet the level of
need existing in each church.

To: Ephesus- "You've lost your first love"
Smyrna – "The Persecuted Church "
Pergamum –"The Compromising Church"
Thyatira-"The Corrupt Church"
Now we come to Sardis-"The Dead Church"

Notice that there is a descending condition of need in each of these church's: From losing their first love to being dead, and worse yet, not ever knowing or realizing it. It is a terrible thing when you become blind to your own circumstances. Remember we've said, "That the greatest deception in life is self-deception" Just when you think you're doing alright without God, Reality is, "You're not!"

Jesus introduces himself, saying, I have the seven spirits of God (Isaiah 11:2-3) and the seven stars in My hand – I know you're Works – You have a name – (that you are Alive but you are Dead) Be watchful/strengthen the little that remains. "I have not found your works to be perfect"

Revelation 3:3
"Remember therefore how you have received and heard; hold fast and repent. Therefore if you will not watch, I will come upon you as a thief, and you will not know what hour I will come upon you."

Today's application to this passage, after serving God a while, many people forget who and what they were before Christ was in their lives. They put those memories behind them and forget that special turning point moment!

Sardis had a false sense of security because they had built a fortress around the city so strong that it seemed impregnable. That when the Persians came against them, they could not get in, they besieged the city and waited. Until one night, one of Cyrus's men saw a soldier who had fallen asleep while on watch on the wall and dropped his helmet outside the city walls, so he went down and opened a secret door got his helmet and went back up. That open door gave Cyrus the answer he needed, he sent some troops to the opposite side of the city, and made a ruckus there, causing attention to that side of the city. When the troops went to defend it, Cyrus went in through that secret door and his soldiers took the city. Just when they thought they were secure and safe they were not!

When people compromise with the world they may feel good and secure especially when the church says nothing about it. But the reality is that,

"It's wrong" Jesus promises a reward to those who overcome– *"They shall walk with me"* – *"I will not blot out their name from the book of life."* – *"I will confess his name before my father and the angels. "*

"Remember when you received and what you heard." We should never forget our turning point moment in life. The Sardis church had compromised with the culture of the day. They went along to get along!
It appears that what Jesus is referring to is that they had compromised the exclusivity of Jesus as the only way to God. Today some believers, when asked "Is Jesus the only way" They answer, "He is for me, I don't know about for others" Leaving some form of doubt for those making the question.

The Church in Sardis had destroyed the only message that could save them. In essence their compromise set them on a collision course with spiritual death.

Today's Application,
You may be walking through the most difficult time in your life when it has become very hard to live out your faith and stand on your core values. I encourage you to read these letters and take heart, don't become discouraged,- Don't give up, -Don't give in, and Don't go along to get along.
Remember that even in a spiritually corrupt and dead church, there was a Godly remnant who were willing to stand and live out their

core values, and because they did, we can and we will thrive also.

(A Christian university was praying for the believers who are suffering persecution in China. They received a message back that asked them not to pray that the persecution stop, but to pray, that they remain faithful to God, In the midst of the persecution. Because they had noticed that where the persecution had stopped Believers were now compromising with the Culture of the Day.)

Jesus closes the letter with these words!:
"You have a few names even in Sardis who have not defiled their garments; and they shall walk with Me in white, for they are worthy. He who overcomes shall be clothed in white garments, and I will not blot out his name from the Book of Life;"

Be an overcomer!
You may be a parent whose children have been influenced by the COTD.
Don't give in, Don't give up. God is still on the Throne.

Casting Crowns wrote a song they entitled <u>*"Slow Fade"*</u> that sheds light on how compromise in our lives eventually leads to death.

"Slow Fade"
The writers took a children's song and made it so relevant to our day!
We don't give ourselves to sin all at once, but one small thought or step at a time.
So small that at times it's hard to even notice.
Yet each step we take further from God, moves us closer to sin and will eventually bring destruction.
So we must do what scripture says, Be vigilant for our enemy walks about like a roaring lion seeking who He is going to destroy.

We are now at Philadelphia - 6th letter The Faithful Church"

We have arrived at Jesus' amazing letter to Philadelphia. It's awesome that in the midst of all the spiritual corruption that existed, Jesus found a faithful congregation. And this is what He writes them:

Revelation 3: 7-13
"And to the angel of the church in Philadelphia write, These things says He who is holy, he who holy, he who is true, "He who has the key of David, He who opens and no one shuts and

shuts and no one opens": I know your works. See, I have set before you an open door, and no one can shut it; for you have a little strength, have kept My word, and have not denied My name.

Indeed I will make those of the synagogue of satan, who say they are Jews and are not, but lie—indeed I will make them come and worship before your feet, and to know that I have loved you. Because you have kept My command to persevere, I also will keep you from the hour of trial which shall come upon the whole world, to test those who dwell on the earth. Behold, I am coming quickly! Hold fast what you have, that no one may take your crown. He who overcomes, I will make him a pillar in the temple of My God, and he shall go out no more. I will write on him the name of My God and the name of the city of My God, the New Jerusalem, which comes down out of heaven from My God. And I will write on him My new name. "He who has an ear, let him hear what the Spirit says to the churches." '

The name Philadelphia literally means "brotherly love" and it describes the Good Will and Fellowship that this Congregation had for one another. In His message, to this Faithful Congregation,

I want to focus on three things that Jesus mentions about them.

1. That they had "little strength." Their strength can be compared to an individual who has had a near death experience on the operating table, but by God's Grace was brought back to life again, though alive that person will still be very weak. The "Church" during the Sardis Period had been dead but had now been "Revived."

I need to explain something here, that will help you understand where I'm going with this message and its Relevance to you and I today.

What Jesus is saying to this Philadelphia church is that He had set before them an "open door of opportunity "that no man would be able to shut. His promise is based on the fact that He has the 'Key' that what "He 'opens', no man can shut; and what He 'shuts' what no man can open."

Unless we know why He says this, we can all come up with a different interpretation, and left without understanding this passage. The believers in Philadelphia were suffering because they had chosen not to give up in the midst of persecution. In the beginning,

Christianity had been accepted as a part of Judaism, But as time went on, the separation between the two faiths became wider.

Ultimately, believers were kicked out of the Synagogue. That put them at risk for their lives. Before this time Christian Jews had been exempt from Emperor worship, but the moment they were kicked out, their names were blotted from the Synagogue Membership Book, making them targets for the Romans to kill, when they would not worship Caesar. They were no longer allowed back into the synagogue, even if they knocked on the door, asking to be allowed in, they were denied entry.

2. Jesus' open door statement also refers to the fact that throughout church history God has opened doors of opportunity for the Church to take the Gospel to the nations. In my lifetime, I have seen two major doors that we've experienced open:

#1 The Hippie Revival That occurred in the late 60s and early 70s, when the Holy Spirit moved greatly Among young people, beginning in the universities and later out on the streets. Everyone from the up and outers to the down and outers were coming to

Christ. The "Jesus Revolution Movie" tells of that revival.

#2. The 2nd door was the collapse of Communist Russia, that allowed Christian organizations to enter that country and preach the Gospel.
Our Church is familiar with George and Jill Rodriguez a couple who pastor in Lake Charles, whom we consider our children and part of our church family. They took the opportunity to walk through that open door and were pastors in Russia for about 10-12 years.

#3. I believe that we are at the Point when the next open door moment is about to happen. I believe that Great Revival is here already, what we must do is just yield ourselves to it.
The spiritually hungry are searching for the opportunity to receive and serve. These opportunities will continue to happen until there is no country in the world where the Gospel has not gone.

Jesus says that he has the Key of David meaning, that He has the power to perform His Will.

#4. Jesus also promises that this church will be kept from the *"hour of temptation"* (this means the tribulation period), that will come upon the entire world. In spirit, the Church of Philadelphia continues to exist today, and while it suffered under "persecution" during the "Period of Smyrna," humanity has yet to suffer a persecution like that which will be experienced on a world-wide scale.

That "hour of temptation" is still in the future and refers to the Great Tribulation that will come just before the return of the Lord, when He comes to set up His Millennial Kingdom.

But His promise to the "Philadelphia Church" is that they will not have to experience or go through the Tribulation, but shall be "caught up" before this great trial?
In church history The Philadelphia Church covers the time period between AD 1750 and AD 1900. But remember that the characteristics of each of these church periods will continue on in the church till the end. This is true of their good (faithfulness) and of their bad (corruption, compromise).

Conclusion :
You may be experiencing aloneness, exclusion like the believers in Philadelphia from certain

circles of friends and activities because of your faith. Yet you have decided to remain a part of the faithful church, with a great door of opportunity before you. In order to continue to remain faithful, we must continue to do what the church did in the beginning. Here's what they did:

Acts 2:41-42

"Then those who gladly received his word were baptized; a that day about three thousand souls were added to them. And they continued steadfastly in the apostles'
doctrine and fellowship, in the breaking of bread, and in prayers."

Acts 2: 46-47

"So continuing daily with one accord in the temple, and breaking bread from house to house, they ate their food with gladness and simplicity of heart, praising God and having favor with all the people. And the Lord added to the church daily those who were being saved."

That's why every church should offer,
1-Fellowship relationships with accountability
2-Solid Biblical teaching and counseling,
3-Ministry opportunities,
4-Biblical education,
5-And so much more!

Because in the end, every one of us wants to hear, our Lord say,

Matthew 25:23,

"Well done, good and faithful servant; you have been faithful over a few things,
I will make you ruler over many things. Enter into the joy of your lord."

We have arrived at the final letter to the Lukewarm Church. – Laodicea
They represent the Perils of Prosperity.

Revelation 3: 14-22

"And to the angel of the church of the Laodiceans write, These things says the Amen, the Faithful and True Witness, the Beginning of the creation of God: "I know your works, that you are neither cold nor hot.
I could wish you were cold or hot. So then, because you are lukewarm, and neither cold nor hot, I will vomit you out of My mouth. Because you say, I am rich, have become wealthy, and have need of nothing'— and do not know that you are wretched, miserable, poor, blind, and naked— I counsel you to buy from Me gold refined in the fire, that you may be rich; and white garments, that you may be clothed, that the shame of your nakedness may not be revealed; and anoint your eyes with eye salve, that you may see. As many as I love, I rebuke and chasten. Therefore be zealous and repent.

Behold, I stand at the door and knock. If anyone hears My voice and opens the door, I will come in to him and dine with him, and he with Me. To him who overcomes I will grant to sit with Me on My throne, as I also overcame and sat down with My Father on His throne. "He who has an ear, let him hear what the Spirit says to the churches."

We come to the close of the 7 letters Jesus sent to these churches. Letters that I feel are needed to be addressed as we enter 2025, in light of all the spiritual and cultural darkness we face as believers, and as a nation. I hope and pray that our study will make a difference your life. So now, let us look into what the letter is saying.

Many people believe that if they just had more money to spend, then they would be able to resolve all of their problems, or if they would just be lucky enough to win the lottery, it would be the greatest blessing of their life. Reality is, "Would it really be the blessing they expect it to be"?

Listen to Jack Whittaker's story, one of many that can be found on this Subject. He begins by saying, "I wish that we had torn the ticket up" Jack was already a millionaire when he won a $315 million in a lottery in West Virginia in

2002. The then-55-year-old West Virginia construction company president claimed he went broke about four years later and lost a daughter and a granddaughter to drug overdoses, which he blamed on the curse of the power ball win, according to ABC News.

"My granddaughter is dead because of the money," he told ABC. "You know, my wife had said she wished that she had torn the ticket up. Well, I wish that we had torn the ticket up, too." Whittaker was also robbed of $545,000 sitting in his car while he was at a strip club eight months after winning the lottery. He said "I just don't like Jack Whittaker.
I don't like the hard heart I've got," I don't like what I've become."
"He's the last person I would have prototyped for going completely crazy but he did," "No question it was because he won the lottery."

Here's another report that says,

"Life after winning the lottery may not stay glamorous forever. Whether they win $500 million or $1 million, about 70 percent of lotto winners lose or spend all that money in five years or less."

Robin Williams the famous comedian once said: "Cocaine is God's way of saying, we are making too much money."

What I'm saying with these stories is that being affluent or rich is not all that people think it is; it has its dangers because in many cases it changes the person, as we will see in this letter.

Through-out human history people have always had a problem with being affluently rich. Because it has a way of giving people - a false sense of security,-become over-confident in self -and have a greater desire to be independent from God. So much so that some people can get to a point, they don't feel a need or a want for God.

The _Laodicean Church_ was a wealthy congregation, it had no need of material things, they had it all.

This caused the members of the church to feel a certain self-sufficiency and an indifference towards serving God. What Jesus is saying to this congregation is, "Your affluence/riches, have caused you to lose your desire, fire, zeal, passion, and need for Me.

So now you are lukewarm, indifferent and you make me sick. I wish that you were hot or cold, I could deal with either of those two conditions but your self-sufficient attitude makes Me want to vomit.

Because you say,

"I am rich and have need of nothing"
Their wealth had blinded them to the reality of their spiritual condition.
Jesus continues and says, *"and do not know that you are wretched, miserable, poor, blind, and naked,"* sad part was they didn't know it!

Laodicea was a rich city because it had been built on the commercial trade route, where all business had to travel. It was a garment manufacturing district that produced and manufactured beautiful black wool. What Jesus was saying, "Church you may wear nice clothing in the natural, but you don't have the spiritual clothing that I can provide you with."

There's a famous quote that goes back to the 1400s, that says "clothes make the man", What Jesus is saying here is, that this is not a true statement on a spiritual level.

Paul explains what our clothing should be:
Ephesians 6: 10-11:
"Finally, my brethren, be strong in the Lord and in the power of His might. Put on the whole armor of God, that you may be able to stand against the wiles of the devil."
Jesus continues, "I counsel you to buy from Me gold refined in the fire"
Laodicea had plenty of material gold, but the gold and riches Jesus is referring to here is their lack of spiritual and personal character development that is produced in our lives, out of humbly and faithfully serving God. Too often people tend to lose sight of what God is doing in and through their faithful service from week to week. He is molding and shaping your character, faithfulness, and commitment level. That in turn will help you navigate the trials of life in your home, marriage, and children.
Genuinely serving God will demand change in your life! Many want to receive salvation, but desire to remain the same person they've been.

Then Jesus says, *"and anoint your eyes with eye salve, that you may see."* Laodicea had a medical facility, which treated eye problems with a special eye salve called Phrygian ointment. It amazes me to see how that in each of these letters, Jesus uses items and terms that every person in the congregation would have understood. Like:

1. Gold, the city was a banking center
2, Eye Salve, they had medical school
3, Clothing, they manufactured wool cloth

He references these things so that every reader in the Church could not miss what the message was saying to them. Jesus closes the letter by saying, "As many as I love, I rebuke and chasten." This is so "On point," because the more affluent/independent a person is, the more difficult it becomes for them to accept correction.

In the Book of Hebrews we find this message, ***Hebrews 12:11***
"Now no chastening seems to be joyful for the present, but painful; nevertheless, afterward it yields the peaceable fruit of righteousness to those who have been trained by it."

If you have ever been corrected, then you know that you have had to deal with your, Anger, how dare that person correct me! Pride, who do they think they are! Or maybe even play the blame game, I did it because, its somebody else's fault, or just excuse yourself by saying, "Others do the same thing" so why should I be any different?"

But when we take time to listen to the rebuke, and apply the message given it will produce Godly character that will honor Him. Laodicea had one major natural problem; it had no source of water of its own, and the water they did have had to be piped in from a mineral infested source. So that whenever peopled cooked with this water it would ruin their food. Mineral infested water that when it arrived it was lukewarm tasted horrible and made them sick.

So Jesus says,
"I could wish you were cold or hot. So then, because you are lukewarm, and neither cold nor hot, I will vomit you out of My mouth."

Jesus took every one of His focal points from their lifestyle.

Application: In the Old Testament, Moses warned the Israelites of the problems they would have to deal with in their prosperity as He brought them into their promised land blessing.

Deuteronomy 8:11-14
"Beware that you do not forget the LORD your God by not keeping His commandments, His

*judgments, and His statutes which I command
you today, lest—when you have eaten and are
full, and have built beautiful houses and dwell in
them; and when your herds and your flocks
multiply, and your silver and your gold are
multiplied, and all that you have is
multiplied; when your heart is lifted up, and you
forget the LORD your God who brought you out
of the land of Egypt, from the house of
bondage;"*

Today, America's heart is prideful, and much of
the Church has the same attitude.
Jesus closes this letter, by painting a word
picture of Himself standing at the door of this
Church knocking.

Revelation 3:20:
*"Behold, I stand at the door and knock. If
anyone hears My voice and opens the door, I will
come in to him and dine with him, and he with
Me."*

It appears that this congregation in their
financial and material inebriation had locked
Him out, or could it be that maybe, Jesus
walked out on His own, because their attitude
and actions were causing Him to want to
vomit. Their dependence on Him was no

longer there, but rather on their wealth, status and possessions.

Today, there are mega-churches in our city and across the nation that have the latest and greatest: Programs for all ages, great sound systems and equipment, age appropriate programs. State of the art buildings, and every amenity possible. Could it be, that one of the reasons they do so well is because that Pastor's message does not offend or correct the congregations compromising lifestyles?

Don't misunderstand I'm not trying to be ultra-religious or sanctimonious or believe that we are better and have it all together! Because we don't. We must always remember, you don't become greater by tearing/putting others down. We are not perfect either!
But, on many occasions these people
are told and made to feel that they are
alright just as they are, but sadly, like the lotto winners, they will end up financially, morally, and eventually spiritually bankrupt also.

This is my final comment on these letters: It is the Laodicean Church Age that will experience the after effects of the rapture, the great tribulation: Many who thought they were ready for Heaven, because they made a onetime decision for Christ but never truly lived the changed life that is expected out of a committed believer. What we all need is to have the message of the following two verses imprinted in our hearts and minds with their insight and understanding.

They actually paint a modern day Mount Carmel confrontational experience between good versus evil, just like in the days of Elijah. I believe that today, we are looking at two sides of the same coin: The future! The end times!
God's word prophesies, that in the Last Days:

2 Timothy 3:1-5
"But know this, that in the <u>last days perilous times</u> will come: For men will be lovers of themselves, lovers of money, boasters, proud, blasphemers, disobedient to parents, unthankful, unholy, unloving, unforgiving, slanderers, without self-control, brutal, despisers of good, traitors, headstrong, haughty, lovers of pleasure rather than lovers of God, having a form of godliness but denying its power.
And from such people turn away!"

That's one side of the coin! Here's the other side:

Acts 2: 17-18

"And it shall come to pass in the last days, says God,
That <u>I will pour out of My Spirit on all flesh</u>;
your sons and your daughters shall prophesy,
your young men shall see visions, your old men
shall dream dreams.
And on My menservants and on My
maidservants I will pour out My Spirit in those
days; And they shall prophesy.

Which last day experience will you and your
families choose to be part of?

As we study these Letters, they have three
levels of application that must be considered
and understood, if not these messages will only
remain information to you.

#1 -These were seven literal churches, some
had positive things happening and most had
negative issues that Jesus said they would have
to deal with. These were churches with great
opportunities and major problems.

#2 - These letters represent 7 categories,
that can describe any church that has ever
existed or that exists today. The question for us
is this; "What kind of church have we (our
generation) decided to be.

By the same token, this principle can also be applied to every individual person, because you may attend a faithful church, but personally decide to live a life of compromise, to the point that you become spiritually dead and not even know it. Today ask yourself, are you a part of the church in Philadelphia, Smyrna, Ephesus, Pergamum of Thyatira or worse yet Sardis or Laodicea?

#3 - These Churches also represent 7 literal periods of church history which are:
A. The Apostolic Church ≈ 30 - 300 A.D.
   (This would include the Ephesian Church)
   who Lost their 1st Love.)
 B. The Martyr Church ≈ 100 - 313 A.D.
    (The Church in Smyrna)
C. The Compromising Church ≈ 314 - 590 A.D. (Church in Pergamum)
D. The Corrupt Church ≈ 590 - 1517 A.D. (Thyatira) Middle Ages
E. The Reformation Church ≈ 1517-1700
   (The Church in Sardis) Dead!
   Martin Luther, John Hus, Polycarp,
F. The Revival Church ≈ 1700-1900
   (The Church of Philadelphia)
G. The Laodicean Church
   (Lukewarm Church/ Prosperous but dead)

It is the Laodicean Church Age that will enter into the tribulation period. While we won't have to go through the tribulation, we will experience some birth pangs much like a mother when she begins to bring forth a child. The child does not come forth immediately yet the pains are very present. Remember Jesus' promise to the Philadelphian Church:

"Because you have kept My command to persevere, I also will keep you from the hour of trial which shall come upon the whole world, to test those who dwell on the earth."

John Experiences God's Throne Room
Chapters 4-5

Revelation 4
Up to now, our focus has been John on the Island of Patmos, but suddenly the camera focus moves *from there into Heaven.*

An open door appears in the Heavens.
John gets to see the throne room of God.

Revelation 4:1
"After these things I looked, and behold, a door standing open in heaven. And the first voice which I heard was like a trumpet speaking with me, saying, "Come up here, and I will show you things which must take place after this."

John explains that the *voice* he heard *sounded* like a Trumpet, his experience is an example of what will happen to the church on *Resurrection Day.*

Paul says: *1 Cor. 15: 51,*
"Behold, I tell you a mystery: We shall not all sleep, but we shall all be changed— in a moment, in the twinkling of an eye, at the last trumpet. For the trumpet will sound, and the dead will be raised incorruptible, and we shall be changed. For this corruptible must put on

incorruption, and this mortal must put on immortality."

John is now in heaven representing the church. The voice tells him: *"I will show you things which must take place after this"* The *question* that arises is *"after what things?"* The Lord felt that this is so *important* that He mentions it *twice in the same verse*, at the beginning and the end. What is this scripture referring to? Remember our three-*part scriptural outline:*

Revelation 1:19.
"Write the things *which you have seen:* Chapter 1 and the things which *are,* Chapter 2-3 and the things *which will take place after this.* Chapter 4-18."

This scripture shows us that we are now entering the *third section* of our *scriptural outline.*
At this point:
1. The *Church Age is now over*
2. The Church has *finished her earthly ministry.*

It is complete and now we begin to see what will happen,

"*Meta Tauta*" *After these things,* Jesus is referring to the things that will happen, *"After the Church Age,"* The *Dispensation of Grace,"* or *After the Rapture of the Church!* Many people have a *problem* with the word "Rapture," because it does *not appear in their* English Bible. But they say this out of *a lack of knowledge.*

In the past, I have for the sake of no room on our electric sign in front of our building, abbreviated Christmas "Xmas." I have received phone calls telling me it's Christmas not Xmas. Well, in *Greek,* the language of the *New Testament,* the word *Christmas begins* with the letter "X," or chi. Much of our English vocabulary comes from the Latin and Greek languages.

For example:
Isaiah 39: 6
'Behold, the days are coming when all that is in your house, and what your fathers have accumulated until this day, <u>shall be carried </u>to Babylon; nothing shall be left,' says the LORD."

I mention this because some of the *King James Bible was* translated from the Greek *Septuagint* Bible.

That Bible translates the word *Rapture* as "*Harpazo*" - Meaning (*To be taken/carried away.*) But there is an *older Spanish translation* called the *Latin Vulgate*. That Bible translated these words as "<u>*Rapto*</u>." So just because we don't see it in our English translation doesn't mean the word does not appear in the Bible.

How will the resurrection take place ?

Scripture says that God is light, Light travels 186,000 miles per second. Earth's Circumference is 24,901 miles. When I use my resurrection illustration at a gravesite service, I give an example of having a weapon that could fire a missile at the speed of light, and that by the time I could take my finger off the trigger that projectile would have travelled seven times around the earth. That's how fast we will be raptured from this earth !

<u>*V.2*</u> John says, "*Immediately I was in the Spirit; and behold, a throne set in heaven, and One sat on the throne*"

He begins to describe the flood of information he was receiving out of his experience in that moment. He begins by describing "*The One who was sitting on the Throne.*"

We may want to see our loved ones when we get to Heaven but *"He who sits on the throne"* will have our complete attention!

Revelation 4:3
"And He who sat there was like a jasper and a sardius stone in appearance; and there was a rainbow around the throne, in appearance like an emerald."

Each stone was projecting its beautiful colors reflected by the light coming from the *"One Sitting on the Throne."* We need to understand that John is restricted in his ability to give us a full explanation of all he is seeing. The best he can do is to frame his explanation with his past experiences. He is describing the Lord, the best way he could. Using the word "Like" as a simile.

Revelation 4: 4
"Around the throne were twenty-four thrones, and on the thrones I saw twenty-four elders sitting, clothed in white robes; and they had crowns of gold on their heads"

Who are these 24 *Elders?*
Who do they represent?
The *Greek word* translated here *as elders,* is,*"Presbuteros."*

This word is *never used* in reference to *angels,* only to describe men, particularly *men of older age* who are mature and able to rule the church. In fact it would be inappropriate to refer to a*ngels as an elder* because an a*ngel never ages.*

Also the *way these elders are dressed* indicate they are men. While angels do appear in white: *White garments* are more commonly attributed to *believers* because, they symbolize *Christ's righteousness* imputed to us at our salvation, by faith alone. According to (***Revelation 3:5, 18; 19:8).***

When the *elders cast their crowns* at the feet of Jesus, they are actually *surrendering* their own *sense of authority.*

Who are they ? It is believed that these elders *represent* the 12 *Tribes of Israel and the 12 apostles* representing *the raptured church.* As they sing songs of redemption (***Rev. 5:8-10)*** They wear their *crowns of victory* and now sit in a place prepared for them by their Redeemer. (***John 14:1-4)***

Although Israel has yet to receive Christ, remember that John is being shown the things that will come "After This" And the Bible says that in the end Israel will be saved. *The golden crowns* worn by the elders also indicate they are men and not angels because crowns are *never promised* to angels, nor are *angels ever seen wearing them.* The word translated "crown" here refers to the *victor's crown,* worn by those who have successfully *completed and won the victory,* as Christ promised. (**Revelation 2:10**; **2 Timothy 4:8**; **James 1:12**).

Paul said it this way,
2 Timothy 4:8
"Finally, there is laid up for me the crown of righteousness, which the Lord, the righteous Judge, will give to me on that Day, and not to me only but also to all who have loved His appearing."

Revelation 4:5
"And from the throne proceeded lightnings, thundering, and voices.
Seven lamps of fire were burning before the throne, which are the seven Spirits of God."

Scripture says that God is light,
1 John 1:5
"This is the message which we have heard from Him and declare to you, that God is light and in Him is no darkness at all."

Who are these 7 Spirits?
The "seven spirits" represent the person of the

Holy Spirit, but the question is why is the number "*Seven*" used to describe Him?
The Bible, and especially the book of Revelation, use the number 7 *to refer to perfection and completion.* John's vision includes a picture *of perfection* and *completeness* in the *Holy Spirit.* And from the beginning, the Bible, identifies the number 7 with something being "*finished*" or "*complete,*" or with *divine perfection.*
 The Bible also mentions,
-*7 Days of Creation*
-*7 Churches Jesus writes to*
-*7 Seals, 7 Trumpets and 7 Bowl Judgments*

Now John mentions the Sea of Glass:
Revelation 4:6-8
"*Before the throne there was a sea of glass, like crystal. And in the midst of the throne, and around the throne, were four living creatures full of eyes in front and in back.*"

What John saw was *impossible* for him to describe, It was *so different from anything he had seen.* To the point that he was compelled to describe it using a *contradictory statement.* Expressing the inexpressible may sometimes demand the use of an oxymoron. A statement that contradicts itself.

How can something be rigid as glass, and still have motion? (Like: Bittersweet and awfully good.) Whatever John saw obviously had both qualities. The motion of the sea and the transparency and purity of the glass.

Then, John explains the four living creatures. There are several different levels of angels some are called Cherubim and others Seraphim. These 4 Angels, because of their closeness to the throne of God, appear to be of the highest rank.

Remember that Ezekiel describes satan as an anointed Cherub.

Ezekiel 28:14
"You were the anointed cherub who covers;
I established you:
You were on the holy mountain of God; you walked back and forth in the midst of fiery stones."

Daniel had a vision of these four beasts. In Ezekiel's vision they had wheels with eyes. Now John has a vision of them also. They each had a similar vision of these anointed Cherubs.

Each one has its own identity,
1. Each had the face a Man
2. Face of Ox
3. Face of a Lion
4. Face of an Eagle

They were depicting the four different ways
that each of the Gospels represent Jesus
1. Mark's Gospel represents Jesus as King
   a Lion
2. Luke - a Lowly servant - Ox
3. Mathew - the Son of Man
4. John - an Eagle

When the prophets described their *visions of the spirit world,* they were also *forced* to use *metaphorical language,* that can be somewhat confusing. *Human language cannot* fully describe *infinite things.* Our minds are too limited to comprehend all the realities of the spiritual realm. But we have this *confidence:* That the *prophets and apostles* wrote under the *inspiration of the Holy Spirit,* and the *words they chose* are the *best possible. Daniel, Ezekiel,* and *John faithfully described* what they saw, and now, we *must faithfully attempt* to *"understand"* their descriptions. For now, *we may not see it all and some of these heavenly things* will still remain mysteries – *until we see* them for ourselves with glorified eyes and minds.

These *Four Living Creatures:* What do they represent? *They are literal beings, a special, exalted order of angels or cherubim.* This is made clear by *their close proximity* to the *throne of God.* (**Ez. 1: 12-20**.) suggests that they are in constant motion around the throne, the *purpose of these four living creatures* also has to do with them

1. Declaring the holiness of God
2. Leading in worship
   A. Adoration of God
   B. And in some way are involved with God's justice.

Because when the Lord *opens* the *first four seals* and sends out the *four horsemen to destroy,* each of these *creature's powerful voices,* sound like *thunder,* As they command John to *"come and see"* (**Rev. 6:1-8**).

The horsemen respond to the words coming from the four powerful creatures, indicating the power that they possess. Their power of authority is seen again in (**Rev. 15:7**) when one of *the four creatures unleashes* the *last seven plagues* of God's wrath on humanity.

Revelation 15:7
"Then one of the four living creatures gave to the seven angel's seven golden bowls full of the wrath of God who lives forever and ever."

These four living creatures are very similar, if not the same, beings that -*Ezekiel* describes - in chaps. 1- 10 and those in **Isaiah 6:1-3.**

They are described as being,
1. -Four in number,
2. -Full of eyes,
3. -Faces like the beings in *Ez. 1:10*
4. -Six wings *Is. 6:2*
5. -Offer worship as the beings in **Is. 6:8**
   saying, *"Holy, holy, holy is the Lord."*

They seem to be involved in *God's divine justice. These elders and creatures appear to worship in tandem.*

Revelation 4: 9-11
"Whenever the living creatures give glory and honor and thanks to Him who sits on the throne, who lives forever and ever, the twenty-four elders fall down before Him who sits on the throne and worship Him who lives forever and ever, and cast their crowns before the throne, saying: "You are worthy, O Lord, To receive glory and honor and power; For You created all

things, And by Your will they exist and were created.”

The *Lamb takes the scroll,* **<u>Revelation 5:1 -3</u>**
“And I saw in the right hand of Him who sat on the throne a scroll written inside and on the back, sealed with seven seals. Then I saw a strong angel proclaiming with a loud voice, “Who is worthy to open the scroll and to lose its seals?” And no one in heaven or on the earth or under the earth was able to open the scroll, or to look at it.”

When John sees Him who sat on the throne He noticed a scroll in his right hand.
What does this scroll represent?
I believe that this is the Title Deed to the world! Remember that when Adam chose to
divorce himself from God and eat of the forbidden fruit. He gave that *title deed*
to satan in the garden. When Satan tempted Jesus in the wilderness he offered Jesus some of it if he would worship only him.

The Scroll is a sealed parchment like paper. When the angel looked for someone who was worthy to open the scroll, and John saw that there was no one, he began to weep.

Revelation 5:4
"So I wept much, because no one was found worthy to open and read the scroll, or to look at it."

One of the elders settled John down,

Revelation 5:5–7
"But one of the elders said to me, "Do not weep. Behold, the Lion of the tribe of Judah, the Root of David, has prevailed to open the scroll and to lose its seven seals.""

So then John, saw Jesus take the scroll, when He took the scroll the 24 elders and the four living creatures all fell before the Lamb and worshipped Him.

Revelation 5:8
"Now when He had taken the scroll, the four living creatures and the twenty-four elders fell down before the Lamb, each having a harp, and golden bowls full of incense, which are the prayers of the saints."

We have all placed prayers before the Lord. The next verses give an answer to what becomes of them.

There will be several groups of victors in Heaven each singing a song of victory.

Revelation 5:9-11

"And they sang a new song, saying:
You are worthy to take the scroll,
And to open its seals; For You were slain and
have redeemed us to God by Your blood Out of
every tribe and tongue and people and nation
And have made us kings and priests to our God;
and we shall reign on the earth." Then I looked,
and I heard the voice of many angels around the
throne, the living creatures, and the elders; and
the number of them was ten thousand times ten
thousand, and thousands of thousands,"

The fact that these *24 Elders were carrying the*
bowls that held the *prayers of the saints* further
proves that these represent *humans and not*
angels.

Revelation 5:12-14

"saying with a loud voice: "Worthy is the Lamb
who was slain to receive power and riches and
wisdom,
And strength and honor and glory and
blessing!"
And every creature which is in heaven and on
the earth and under the earth and such as are in
the sea, and all that are in them, I heard saying:
"Blessing and honor and glory and power be to

Him who sits on the throne, And to the Lamb, forever and ever!" Then the four living creatures said, "Amen!" And the twenty-four elders fell down and worshiped Him."

The Bible says that not only our prayers are heard and stored, but scripture also mentions that even the tears we have shed are stored in His presence. They are kept (In God's tear bottle). God has a tear bottle for us, King David said:

Psalms 56:8
"You number my wanderings; Put my tears into Your bottle; are they not in Your book?"

God is aware of our every prayer. Some prayers He answers immediately, others He will answer later and still others we will find His plan and purpose for them in His presence.

Conclusion: God has:
1. -Given - His only Son
2. -Provided- Forgiveness of Sin, and a way out through Jesus
3. -Protected us- From the Evil one
4. -Warned - Of the impending judgment to come
5. -Prepared - A heavenly home for us
6. -Loved - us unconditionally

7. -Patiently waits - beyond human ability

So then knowing that _His judgments are coming,_

Peter asks this question.
2 Peter 3:11
"Therefore, since all these things will be dissolved, what manner of persons ought you to be in holy conduct and godliness,"

God's Judgment Begins!
Our passage of study in this chapter, will speak of seals and horseman.
They represent: "God's Judgment" upon an unrepentant world, who has rejected His Son.

These are the four horsemen of the apocalypse, four biblical figures who appear in the Book of Revelation. They are revealed by the breaking of the first four of _seven seals._ Each of them represents a _different judgment_ during the tribulation.

Their names are:
1. Conquest
2. War
3. Famine
4. Death

The Seal Judgements
Chapter 6

Revelation. 6: 1-2 First Seal Opened
_"Now I saw when the Lamb opened one of the
seals; and I heard one of the four living
creatures saying with a voice like thunder,
"Come and see." And I looked, and behold,
a white horse. He who sat on it had a bow; and a
crown was given to him, and he went
out conquering and to conquer."_

This white horse rider represents _"conquest."_
He has often been mistaken by many to be
Jesus Christ, but he is not, this is the _antichrist._
He is the pretender of Jesus. (_Anti means
instead of_ or _pretender.)_
He will come dressed up like a _man of peace,_ at
the beginning of the tribulation. He will be
given Satan's power to deceive.
The a_nti-christ_ will begin by entering into a
peace treaty with Israel for the first _3 1/2 years
of the tribulation._ He will help Israel rebuild
the temple.

According to
Dan, 8:25:
_It will be," Through his cunning he shall
cause deceit to prosper under his rule; And he_

shall exalt himself in his heart. He shall destroy many in their prosperity.
He shall even rise against the prince of princes; but he shall be broken without human means."

In the middle of the 7 years he will break his agreement with Israel and perform the abomination *of desolation. What is this abomination?*
According to the Book of Daniel, it is the celebration of pagan sacrifices with which the Seleucid King *Antiochus Epiphanes IV* celebrated in the Temple in 167 BC. (His self-given title of *Epiphanes* meant *"God Manifest"*) But the Jews called him *"Epimanes"* meaning *"Mad One."*

Antiochus Invaded the Jewish Temple in Jerusalem;
1.-Set an altar to Zeus, the Greek god.
2.-He sacrificed a pig on the altar something that is forbidden by Jewish law.
3.-When the Jews expressed their anger he had many killed.
4.-He declared circumcision to be illegal.
5.-Ordered that the people worship foreign gods.
6.-He set himself up to be worshipped as a god.

All of this is just a foretaste of what the anti-christ will do.

<u>Revelation 6: 3-4. (Then the 2nd Seal was opened)</u>
"When He opened the second seal, I heard the second living creature saying, "Come and see." Another horse, fiery red, went out and it was granted to the one who sat on it to take peace from the earth, and that people should kill one another; and there was given to him a great sword."

This 2nd horseman – Is the Red horse rider. He represents "War," he will take peace from the earth and bring destruction. Here we can see the difference between Jesus and this 2nd horseman.

1. When Jesus came, the announcement given was that *He brought Peace on Earth.*
2. The second horseman *will take peace from the earth.* Nation will war against nation.

<u>The question is: What is holding the anti-christ and these things from occurring, Now?</u>

2 Thessalonians 2:7-8

"For the mystery of lawlessness is already at work; only he who now restrains will do so until he is taken out of the way. And then the lawless one will be revealed whom the Lord will consume with breath of His mouth and destroy with the brightness of His coming."

This restraining force on the earth is the Church. (It is you and I?) We are that force holding him back! As bad as evil may be today, it is nothing compared to what it will be once the church is gone. The reason that things on earth are not worse than they are it is because of us the believers.

We are the restraining force and the conscience of the nation in the world keeping evil at bay. Imagine for a moment if we were not here, representing a Godly conscience, a moral lifestyle, and holding back ungodliness from ruling.

So let us continue to be salt and light in the world. Salt stimulates thirst in people. We must cause others to thirst for God. We are to be light in a dark sin filled world showing them the path to the cross.

Then the 3rd Seal is opened, the 3rd horseman is the black horse rider. He will bring "scarcity and famine" that rationing will be forced upon people.

Rev. 6:5-6

"When He opened the third seal, I heard the third living creature say, "Come and see." So I looked, and behold, a black horse, and he who sat on it had a pair of scales in his hand. And I heard a voice in the midst of the four living creatures saying, "A quart of wheat for a denarius, and three quarts of barley for a denarius; and do not harm the oil and the wine."

What this passage is saying, is that *"a quart of wheat will cost one days wage"*

Dramatic lack and inflation will be experienced. There will be great hunger across the globe as has never been seen. How will this happen?
It could be as a result of the:
1. -Affects of Nuclear War
2.-Drought
3.-Hoarding- There will be some who because of their wealth, will still have something to eat. But the crowds of people won't.

The good news is that during all of this, we will already be in heaven. If you are a believer!

During the tribulation, the anti-Christ will help Israel rebuild the temple as a gesture of goodwill, but in the middle of the tribulation he will set himself up as God. He will make an image of himself and expect the world to worship him. This is what Daniel calls the *abomination of desolation.*

In **_Matt. 24_** Jesus speaks of the "_Signs of the Times_" He mentions the tribulation and refers to Daniel's prophecy in his message in the _Olivet Discourse._
The prophet Daniel mentioned the abomination of desolation in three places:

1, _Daniel 9:27:_
"Then he shall confirm a covenant with many for one week: But in the middle of the week He shall bring an end to sacrifice and offering. And on the wing of abominations shall be one who makes desolate, Even until the consummation, which is determined is poured out on the desolate."

2, _Dan. 11:31_
"Forces shall be mustered by him, and they shall defile the sanctuary fortress; then they shall take away the daily sacrifices, and place *there* the abomination of desolation."

3, Dan. 12:11

"From the time that the regular sacrifice is abolished and the abomination of desolation is set up, there will be 1,290 days" (3 1/2 years).

The Anti-Christ will:
2 Thessalonians 2:4

"who opposes and exalts himself above all that is called God or that is worshiped, so that he sits as God in the temple of God, showing himself that he is God."

God's warning says,
Zechariah 12:3

"On that day I will make Jerusalem a heavy stone for all the peoples. All who lift it will surely hurt themselves and all the nations of the earth will gather against it."

We must realize that Jerusalem is the epicenter of all end-time events, when you see things happening on the world's stage, look at how it affects Israel.

The book of Revelation guarantees us, one thing, that in the end, *"All BELIEVERS WILL WIN!"* Now, there will be many who will receive Jesus as Lord during the tribulation. Great revival will happen but at the cost of their lives...

Many believe that in the resurrection, that it is the Holy Spirit whom will be taken away from the earth, That is wrong! That is impossible! It is the CHURCH that will be taken according to

1 Thessalonians 4: 16-18
"For the Lord Himself will descend from heaven with a shout, with the voice of an archangel, and with the trumpet of God. And the dead in Christ will rise first. Then we who are alive and remain shall be caught up together with them in the clouds to meet the Lord in the air. And thus we shall always be with the Lord. Therefore comfort one another with these words."

The Holy Spirit must remain on Earth for revival to take place.
Without the Holy Spirit, revival can NOT happen!
Then the 4th Seal will be opened. This is the pale horse rider who represents "Death and Hades."

Rev. 6:7-8
"When He opened the fourth seal, I heard the voice of the fourth living creature saying, "Come and see." So I looked, and behold, a pale horse. And the name of him who sat on it was Death, and Hades followed with him. And power was

given to them over a fourth of the earth, to kill with sword, with hunger, with death, and by the beasts of the earth."

And they will have power to kill with the sword and with hunger a *"fourth part"* of the earth's *population.*

The word "pale" is the Greek word "chloros" It is pale green in color, and it represents illness and death. Where have we heard that word "chloros" before? Clorox and what color is it? It is also pale green in color and if you consume it, you won't live very long.

Now let's figure if *1/4 of the population* will be lost.
(*In 2020 it was estimated that we had 7.8 Billion in population*). Today the world's population probably sits right at about eight Billion. So that means that two *Billion people will perish,* when this seal is broken. The famine caused by the previous horseman will cause a great *pestilence* that the *wild birds and beasts* will make the death of humanity their *call to dinner. That marks the end of the 4 horseman. but there are still 3 Seals left.*
Then the *5th Seal* will be opened and *the cry of the martyrs* will be heard.

Revelation 6:9-11

"When He opened the fifth seal, I saw under the altar the souls of those who had been slain for the word of God and for the testimony which they held. and they cried with a loud voice, saying, "How long, O Lord, holy and true, until You judge and avenge our blood on those who dwell on the earth?" Then a white robe was given to each of them; and it was said to them that they should rest a little while longer, until both the number of their fellow servants and their brethren, who would be killed as they were, was completed."

These are none other than the tribulations saints. Men, Women, and Children who will be killed for their faith in Christ, and their unwillingness to take the mark of the beast. They are asking for God's judgment to be given to their murderers. His answer to them is not now, there are more who must die for their faith.

Then the Sixth Seal will be opened, It will cause great cosmic disturbances

Revelation 6: 12-17.

"I looked when He opened the sixth seal, and behold, there was a great earthquake; and the

sun became black as sackcloth of hair, and the moon became like blood.

And the stars of heaven fell to the earth, as a fig tree drops its late figs when it is shaken by a mighty wind. Then the sky receded as a scroll when it is rolled up, and every mountain and island was moved out of its place. And the kings of the earth, the great men, the rich men, the commanders, the mighty men, every slave and every free man, hid themselves in the caves and in the rocks of the mountains, and said to the mountains and rocks, "Fall on us and hide us from the face of Him who sits on the throne and from the wrath of the Lamb! For the great day of His wrath has come, and who is able to stand?"

Note,

The effects of this Seal will begin with a world-wide earthquake so powerful that it will affect the Heavens. Asteroids and Meteors will rain down upon the earth. Men will run and hide for fear, crying out to nature to hide and protect them from God's anger.

Yet, there is still no mention of their repentance! There was a News Report on ABC: "On *February 15, 2013,* that an asteroid slammed into the Earth's atmosphere at nearly 70,000 kilometers per hour. (*43,496 miles per hour*) Almost the size of a tennis court, it blazed brilliantly in the sky as if it were a second sun. All of this happened in mere seconds, with the ultimate blow occurring when the asteroid was about 30 kilometers up. The energy of its last motion was converted into heat in an instant. The resulting huge fireball briefly outshone the sun in the sky, emitting energy equivalent to the detonation of about half a million metric tons of TNT."

So let's ask Peter's question again,
2 Peter 3:11
"Therefore, since all these things will be dissolved, what manner of persons ought you to be in holy conduct and godliness."

There is a theological term introduced in the following chapters it is called "Parenthetical"

We have seen 6 Seals opened, there is one left.

Now we enter chapter 7, it is called "parenthetical" It is an insert or further explanation to what has already been said. It gives more information about the first 6 Seals that have already been broken. One thing that will happen during this time is that there will be a great revival.

Revival will Come !

The 144,00 Witnesses
Chapter 7

Revelations 7: 1-3

"After these things I saw four angels standing at the four corners of the earth, holding the four winds of the earth, that the wind should not blow on the earth, on the sea, or on any tree.
***V.2** Then I saw another angel ascending from the east, having the seal of the living God. And he cried with a loud voice to the four angels to whom it was granted to harm the earth and the sea, **v.3**, saying,*
"Do not harm the earth, the sea, or the trees till we have sealed the servants of our God on their foreheads."

These four angels are about to release winds of destructive force upon the earth. But God restrains them from doing so until His servants were sealed on their foreheads. But this angel holds them back from harming the earth and sea, until the rest of servants of God are sealed. But the winds that will be released will have hurricane and tornado level force during the great tribulation. But before this happens God wants His servants to be sealed first. Who are these Servants? (Tribulation Saints), What is this Seal? We don't know, God did not explain it! So we won't either.

Revelation 7:4
"And I heard the number of those who were sealed. One hundred and forty-four thousand of all the tribes of the children of Israel were sealed:"

During the tribulation -there will be 144,000 *Jewish evangelists* that will be raised up to point the Jewish nation to Christ. (These 144,000 are not Jehovah's Witnesses nor are they the World-Wide Church of God!) These will be Jewish people.

Revelation 7:4-8
"And I heard the number of those who were sealed one hundred and forty-four thousand of all the tribes of the children of Israel were sealed:" of the tribe of Judah twelve thousand were sealed; of the tribe of Reuben twelve thousand were sealed;
Gad twelve thousand were sealed; Asher twelve thousand were sealed;
Naphtali twelve thousand were sealed; Manasseh twelve thousand were sealed;
Simeon twelve thousand were sealed; Levi twelve thousand were sealed;
Issachar twelve thousand were sealed; Zebulun twelve thousand were sealed;
Joseph twelve thousand were sealed; Benjamin twelve thousand were sealed."

Notice: that the Tribe of Dan and Ephraim are not included although they are mentioned later.

These 144,000 will bring Israel to the Lord? And they will bring revival across the world. God allows John to see the end from the beginning.

The Tribulation Saints
Rev. 7: 9-17.

"After these things I looked, and behold, a great multitude which no one could number, of all nations, tribes, peoples, and tongues, standing before the throne and before the Lamb, clothed with white robes, with palm branches in their hands, and crying out with a loud voice, saying, "Salvation belongs to our God who sits on the throne, and to the Lamb!"
All the angels stood around the throne and the elders and the four living creatures, and fell on their faces before the throne and worshiped God, saying:"Amen! Blessing and glory and wisdom, thanksgiving and honor and power and might be to our God forever and ever. Amen."Then one of the elders answered, saying to me, "Who are these arrayed in white robes, and where did they come from?" And I said to him, "Sir, you know." So he said to me, "These are the ones who come out of the great tribulation, and washed their

robes and made them white in the blood of the Lamb. Therefore they are before the throne of God and serve Him day and night in His temple. And He who sits on the throne will dwell among them. They shall neither hunger anymore nor thirst anymore; the sun shall not strike them, nor any heat; for the Lamb who is in the midst of the throne will shepherd them and lead them to living fountains of waters. And God will wipe away every tear from their eyes."

These are none other than the tribulations saints! The obvious observation for us is that they didn't have to go through that. They could have gone up in the rapture, but they chose to reject Jesus, but ultimately received Him at the cost of their lives.

From Seal to Trumpet Judgements
Chapters 8-9

The 7th seal becomes the announcement of the seven trumpets.

In the last two chapters we experienced the opening of the first 6 Seals, each will bring an expression of God's judgment on an unrepentant world. Now we will look into the 7th Seal that gives way for the next segment of God's judgment. The sounding of the 7 trumpets. Here they are used to announce God's judgment on an unrepentant world.

The 7th seal will be opened and the seven trumpets will begin to sound.

Revelation 8:1 -13
"When He opened the seventh seal, there was silence in heaven for about half an hour. And I saw the seven angels who stand before God and to them were given seven trumpets."

Try being silent for about 30 seconds then watch the effect that it has on those around you!

Silence can be a very impactful experience. It is reminiscent of the silence practiced by Israel as the priest entered the holy place to offer incense before the Lord. While the people wondered whether the priest would live or die in God's Holy presence. We can't begin to imagine the silence among a multitude of millions before the Lord. But after these things, all Hell will break loose!

V.3-6

"Then another angel, having a golden censer, came and stood at the altar. He was given much incense that he should offer it with the prayers of all the saints upon the golden altar which was before the throne. And the smoke of the incense, with the prayers of the saints, ascended before God from the angel's hand. Then the angel took the censer, filled it with fire from the altar, and threw it to the earth. And there were noises, thunderings, lightning, and an earthquake. So the seven angels who had the seven trumpets prepared themselves to sound."

The incense represents our prayers, they go up before God's throne and become a beautiful, sweet fragrance, as the angel placed them on the altar. Understand that God loves it when we talk to Him.

Then the angel took the same censer and took fire from the altar and poured it out on earth that caused thunderings, lightnings, and an earthquake to happen.

Then the First Trumpet Sounded.

In the book of ***Numbers 10: 1-10,***
God gave Israel instructions on the use of trumpets. They were to be used practically to make special announcements like:
1.-Calling an assembly.
2.-To sound an alarm.
3.-To call troops into battle.

Here they are used to announce
God's impending judgment:

First Trumpet: The vegetation will be struck

Revelation 8:7
"The first angel sounded: And hail and fire followed, mingled with blood, and they were thrown to the earth. And a third of the trees were burned up, and all green grass was burned up."

It was vegetation that God created first so it will be the first to be affected by His judgment.

Second Trumpet: The Seas are Struck

Revelation 8:8-9
"Then the second angel sounded: And something like a great mountain burning with fire was thrown into the sea, and a third of the sea became blood. And a third of the living creatures in the sea died, and a third of the ships were destroyed."

Could that be an asteroid, falling from the Heavens? This will destroy 1/3 of all living creatures, 1/3 of all ships in the Sea.

Third Trumpet: The Waters are Struck

Revelation 8:10-11
"Then the third angel sounded: And a great star fell from heaven, burning like a torch, and it fell on a third of the rivers and on the springs of water. The name of the star is Wormwood. A third of the waters became wormwood, and many men died from the water, because it was made bitter."

Wormwood was a well-known bitter herb in Bible times, so by naming the star wormwood, it informs us of its effect; it will embitter the fresh waters of the earth to a degree that the water will be undrinkable. Wormwood is only mentioned here in the New Testament, but it is mentioned several times in the Old Testament.

It is peculiar that these judgments will be fulfilled in thirds, Could it be that God's mercy and grace continues to be expressed, giving people an opportunity to repent.

Fourth Trumpet: The Heavens are Struck

Revelation 8:12
"Then the fourth angel sounded: And a third of the sun was struck, a third of the moon, and a third of the stars, so that a third of them were darkened. A third of the day did not shine, and likewise the night."

(If you remember the news reports of the effects of Mt. St. Helens volcano ,when it exploded in 1980, how it clouded the skies in Washington State for days, this catastrophe will have a similar affect, only World-wide.)

It appears that the *Fourth Trumpet* is an announcement made by the loud voice of an

angel, declaring the (Woes) or horrors of the
5th, 6th, and 7th Trumpets;

Revelation 8:13
*"And I looked, and I heard an angel flying
through the midst of heaven, saying with a loud
voice, "Woe, woe, woe to the inhabitants of the
earth, because of the remaining blasts of the
trumpet of the three angels who are about to
sound!"*

He is announcing the *Three Woes*. And again
we see this pattern of *destruction in thirds*,
God still giving man an opportunity to repent.
God has so much Love and Patience towards
humanity.

Let's explain the WOES. "The judgments of
these last three trumpets will be produced as
well as filled by *demonic forces* intensified to
greater and greater tormenting power on the
earth dwellers. "*Dr. Elizabeth Williams,
Prevision of History*"

A *woe in the Bible* refers to grief, anguish,
affliction, wretchedness, calamity, or trouble. It
can be used as an exclamation of judgment on
others, like, "Woe to Him, if he does that
again." It can also describe a condition of deep

suffering from misfortune, ruinous trouble and economic woes.

The Fifth Trumpet
The Locusts from the Bottomless Pit will be released and bring the first woe:

Revelation 9:1 -6
*"Then the fifth angel sounded: And I saw
a star fallen from heaven to the earth.
To him was given the key to the bottomless
pit. And he opened the bottomless pit, and
smoke arose out of the pit like the smoke of a
great furnace. So the sun and the air were
darkened because of the smoke of the pit. Then
out of the smoke locusts came upon the earth.
And to them was given power, as the scorpions
of the earth have power. They were commanded
not to harm the grass of the earth, or any green
thing, or any tree, but only those men who do
not have the seal of God on their foreheads.
"And they were not given authority to kill them,
but to torment them for (five months). Their
torment was like the torment of a scorpion when
it strikes a man. In those days men will seek
death and will not find it; they will desire to die,
and death will flee from them."*

Scripture is clear as to who this Star falling
from Heaven is, he is none other than Satan

himself, the evil one. Jesus will give him the keys to open the Abuso. These demonic creatures will come forth in the form of locusts. They are described as having hair like women, and their teeth were like lions' teeth and breastplates like iron, they are sent to harm those who have not been sealed, to torment but not kill them, for a period of 5 months. Death will not be possible at this time. Man will try to die, but they won't be able to. Still man will not call on God! The devil will be confined to this bottomless pit when Jesus returns to set up His Kingdom. (**_Rev. 20:1_**)

Scripture mentions the bottomless pit but there are other words that are translated Hell in the Bible, that unless you have a Strong's Concordance you won't know which of the words is being used.

What are they and what is their purpose? Before Jesus died on the cross, everyone who died went to the same place, called Hades or Sheol it was divided into two divisions: Abrahams Bosom was a place of peace, rest, and joy, in other words, it was Paradise. Jesus told the thief dying at His side, _"Today you will be with me in Paradise"_ The other compartment of Sheol was a place of torment.

Sheol is the word used in the Old Testament and it means a place for the dead or the departed souls.

Hades is the Greek word used in the New Testament.

It is the equivalent for Sheol.

Both of these terms represent a place both of rest and torment. We see this illustrated in **Luke 16:23** with the story that Jesus tells of the of the rich man and Lazarus experience at death.

Gehenna. Jesus also uses this term in **Matthew 5:29**

"If your right eye causes you to sin, pluck it out and cast it from you; for it is more profitable for you that one of your members perish, than for your whole body to be cast into hell."

Jesus was referring to the Ge-Hinnom valley that is south of Jerusalem. It was a place designated for trash and at one point in Jerusalem's history was a place used for child sacrifice. Jesus refers to it as a place of judgment after death.

Bottomless Pit/Abyss (Abuso). This is like a holding tank for a certain type of demonic creatures that will be released to torture an unrepentant world mentioned here in

<u>*Rev. 9: 1-12.*</u> It is also the place where Satan will be held during the millennial reign.

<u>Revelation 20: 1-3</u>
"Then I saw an angel coming down from heaven, having the key to the bottomless pit and a great chain in his hand. He laid hold of the dragon, that serpent of old, who is the Devil and Satan, and bound him for a thousand years and he cast him into the bottomless pit, and shut him up, and set a seal on him, so that he should deceive the nations no more till the thousand years were finished. But after these things he must be released for a little while."

The Bottomless Pit is associated with another word "<u>*Tartarus*</u>" it used to describe a place of judgment.

Peter uses it in:
<u>*2 Peter 2:4*</u>
"For if God did not spare the angels who sinned, but cast them down to hell (Tartarus) and delivered them into chains of darkness, to be reserved for judgment;"

<u>*Lake of Fire*</u>:
It is the final destination of punishment for all beings human and angelic who rejected God's Plan of the Ages.

Revelation 20: 14-15

"Then death and Hades were cast into the lake of fire. This is the second death and anyone not found written in the Book of Life was cast into the lake of fire."

Revelation 9: 7-11

"The shape of the locusts was like horses prepared for battle. On their heads were crowns of something like gold, and their faces were like the faces of men. They had hair like women's hair, and their teeth were like lions' teeth. And they had breastplates like breastplates of iron, and the sound of their wings was like the sound of chariots with many horses running into battle. They had tails like scorpions, and there were stings in their tails. Their power was to hurt men five months. And they had as king over them the angel of the Bottomless Pit, whose name in Hebrew is Abaddon, but in Greek he has the name Apollyon."

Again we must remember that John is speaking metaphorically, doing the best he can to describe creatures and things he has never seen, with words that come from his limited vocabulary. Just think about how you would have described these creatures. Thank God for the Holy Spirit's help.

Revelation 9:12

"One woe is past behold; still two more woes are coming after these things."

Sixth Trumpet: **The angels from the Euphrates are released,**

Revelation 9: 13-21

"Then the sixth angel sounded: And I heard a voice from the four horns of the golden altar, which is before God, saying to the sixth angel who had the trumpet. "Release the four angels who are bound at the great river Euphrates." So the four angels, who had been prepared for the hour and day and month and year, were released to kill a third of mankind. Now the number of the army of the horsemen was two hundred million; I heard the number of them. And thus I saw the horses in the vision: those who sat on them had breastplates of fiery red, hyacinth blue, and sulfur yellow; and the heads of the horses were like the heads of lions; and out of their mouths came fire, smoke, and brimstone. By these three plagues a third of mankind was killed—by the fire and the smoke and the brimstone which came out of their mouths. For their power is in their mouth and in their tails; for their tails are like serpents, having heads; and with them they do harm.

But the rest of mankind, who were not killed by these plagues, did not repent of the works of their hands, that they should not worship demons, and idols of gold, silver, brass, stone, and wood, which can neither see nor hear nor walk. And they did not repent of their murders or their sorceries or their sexual immorality or their thefts."

That voice that was heard had to be God's voice.
Who were these four angels?
They don't appear to be identified. Their mission was to kill 1/3 of mankind, and after all that mortality, man still hardens his heart and does not repent of his sin. Sin causes the hardening of the heart instead of giving freedom, habitual sin produces an enslaved consciousness. We can understand its powerful grip when we compare it to chemical addiction, the chronic use of drugs, causes a hardening of the heart. When man hardens his heart he is without hope and without God in this world.

The voice giving the order came from the altar before God's presence.
What do these four horns represent?
These were horn-like projections protruding from the four corners of the altar of burnt

offering. As per God's instructions for the altar's construction in (**_Ex. 27:2_**).

In the Bible horns are a symbol of God's Mercy strength, and victory when He delivers a person.

First Kings tells the story of King David's selection of Solomon to succeed him on the throne, his other son Adonijah had already declared and celebrated himself as king.

So when he found out of David's decision. He became fearful of his brother, so he ran to the altar and took hold of the horns.

1 Kings 1:50

"Now Adonijah was afraid of Solomon; so he arose, and went and took hold of the horns of the altar."

1 Kings 1:52

Then Solomon said, "If he proves himself a worthy man, not one hair of him shall fall to the earth; but if wickedness is found in him, he shall die."

This action provided him amnesty, for what he had done.

The four demonic angels. These are probably the angel's reserved in everlasting chains of darkness until the great Day of Judgment, mentioned in:

2 Peter 2:4
"For if God did not spare the angels who sinned, but cast them down to hell and delivered them into chains of darkness, to be reserved for judgment;"

Jude 1:6
"And the angels who did not keep their proper domain, but left their own abode, He has reserved in everlasting chains under darkness for the judgment of the great day;"

These have been incarcerated for the sake of humanities protection. But scripture makes it clear that these are evil creatures that will be released and used as instruments of God's judgment.
They will unleash great plagues upon the earth. And still man will not repent; his heart will be hardened by the sin that enslaves him.

So let's ask Peter's question one more time.
2 Peter 3:11
"Therefore, since all these things will be dissolved, what manner of persons ought you to be in holy conduct and godliness?"

The Mighty Angel and the Little Book
Revelation 10-11.

Rev. 10: 1-3

"I saw still another mighty angel coming down from heaven, clothed with a cloud. And a rainbow was on his head; his face was like the sun, and his feet like pillars of fire. He had a little book open in his hand. And he set his right foot on the sea and his left foot on the `land, and cried with a loud voice, as when a lion roars. When he cried out, seven thunders uttered their voices."

We encounter another parenthetical message here, What does that mean?

Parenthetical passages explain experiences' that will happen alongside the previous chapters but are not explained in the revealing of the seal, trumpet or bowl judgments. These passages are often misunderstood, causing confusion. This information is necessary in order to bring the reader up to date on what else took place during the fulfillment of these judgments in Revelation.

Now let us look into these first three verses, John sees a mighty angel coming down from Heaven.

The term angel here is used to describe an office not just the spiritual qualities of a being. The word angel means messenger of God, and they are often described having human form with wings.
The word angel also suggests goodness and is often used to refer to someone who gives comfort and aid to others in times of trouble.

The movie "Ordinary Angel "is the true story of woman who goes out of her way to help a family. Now, as a child you may have appeared to look like an innocent angel; but as we all know appearances are deceiving at times.

The term angel is also used of Jesus, in several passages,
Matthew 1:24
"Then Joseph, being aroused from sleep, did as the angel of the Lord commanded him and took to him his wife,"

The Angel mentioned here in **_Rev. 10,_** is none other than Jesus, He is:
1. Clothed with cloud, rainbow on his head
2. Face like a sun
3. Set his right foot on the sea
4. Left foot on the land
5. He had a little book open in His hand
6. His voice was compared to that of a Lion.

Only Jesus can have this kind of power and ability!

Remember what the Elder told John,
Revelation 5:5
"But one of the elders said to me, "Do not weep. Behold, the Lion of the tribe of Judah, the Root of David, has prevailed to open the scroll and to loose its seven seals."

When the Angel spoke,
Revelation 10: 4
"When he cried out, (The) seven thunders uttered their voices. Now when the seven thunders uttered their voices, I was about to write; but I heard a voice from heaven saying to me, "Seal up the things which the seven thunders uttered, and do not write them."

John was about to begin writing, what they were saying, But he was told not to write anything they spoke. So then because John didn't write anything, we can't comment on it either. One day we will all be told what they said!

Revelation 10: 5-7
"The angel (Jesus) whom I saw standing on the sea and on the land raised up his hand to heaven and swore by Him who lives forever and

ever, who created heaven and the things that are in it, the earth and the things that are in it, and the sea and the things that are in it, that there should be delay no longer, but in the days of the sounding of the seventh angel, when he is about to sound, the mystery of God would be finished, as He declared to His servants the prophets."

This passage mentions that the angel swore, just as God did with Abraham recorded in:

Hebrews 6:13
"For when God made a promise to Abraham, because He could swear by no one greater, He swore by Himself,"

Then John was commanded to eat the little book in
Revelation 10: 8-9
"Then the voice which I heard from heaven spoke to me again and said, "Go, take the little book which is open in the hand of the Angel who stands on the sea and on the earth. "So I went to the Angel and said to him, "Give me the little book." And He said to me, "Take and eat it; and it will make your stomach bitter, but it will be as sweet as honey in your mouth."

Have you ever heard someone tell of a bitter/sweet experience they had, this is what happened to John,

_V.10_

"Then I took the little book out of the Angel's hand and ate it, and it was as sweet as honey in my mouth.

John was told to eat the book; this is the same book we saw back in Chapter 5,

It represents the Title Deed of the Earth.

Revelation 5:1

"And I saw in the right hand of Him who sat on the throne a scroll (Book) written inside and on the back, sealed with seven seals."

When John ate the book, at first it tasted sweet and good, to consume, but because of the end results, John goes on to explain,

_V.10-11_

"But when I had eaten it, my stomach became bitter. And he said to me, "You must prophesy again about many peoples, nations, tongues, and kings."

But when John had to digest physically and emotionally what the world and humanity will have to go through to get God's ultimate result, his experience became bitter.

The Two Witnesses
Chapter 11

This continues the parenthesis, that began in chapter ten.

John continues to share his experience:
Rev. 11:1-3
"Then I was given a reed like a measuring rod. And the angel stood, saying, "Rise and measure the temple of God, the altar, and those who worship there. But leave out the court, which is outside the temple, and do not measure it, for it has been given to the Gentiles. And they will tread the holy city underfoot for forty-two months. And I will give power to my two witnesses, and they will prophesy one thousand two hundred and sixty days, clothed in sackcloth."

These prophesies are based on the Babylonian calendar year of 360 days. Three and a half years would be 1260 days. They did not have the Gregorian calendar of today.

Let us use our hands and arms to best understand the opening statement of this chapter.
"I was given a _reed_ like a measuring rod"
A reed, was a measuring stick, much like a yard

stick of today, A reed is a part of the Jewish weights and measures used in John's day.
A _span_ is the measurement between your little finger and your thumb, somewhere between 9-10." _A cubit_, Is the distance between the tip of your middle finger and your elbow,
(around 18-20"). A reed is six cubits long or about 9 feet.

John was told to measure the temple only! The Greek word used here is "naos" and not "hieron" which refers to the entire temple complex. Including the court yard, he was told to only measure the Temple area. This is very important, as you will see later.

This brings us to Daniel's 70 Week Prophecy, What some scholars would call the most important date in history.

Daniel 9: 24-27
"_Seventy weeks are determined for your people and for your holy city, to finish the transgression,to make an end of sins, to make reconciliation for iniquity, to bring in everlasting righteousness, to seal up vision and prophecy, and to anoint the Most Holy. Know therefore and understand that from the going forth of the command to restore and build Jerusalem until Messiah the Prince, there shall_

be seven weeks and sixty-two weeks; the street shall be built again, and the wall, even in troublesome times. And after the sixty-two weeks Messiah shall be cut off, but not for Himself; and the people of the prince who is to come shall destroy the city and the sanctuary. The end of it shall be with a flood, and till the end of the war desolations are determined. Then he shall confirm a covenant with many for one week; but in the middle of the week He shall bring an end to sacrifice and offering. And on the wing of abominations shall be one who makes desolate, even until the consummation, which is determined, is poured out on the desolate."

Daniel's Prophecy says that from the time that King Cyrus' decree went out to restore and rebuild Jerusalem until the day that Jesus would ride into Jerusalem, on Palm Sunday there would be 69 weeks of years totaling = 483 years.

But the Angel told Daniel that there would be 70 weeks, which means that there still remains one week of 7 years left to fulfill God's covenant with Israel. This week of years will take place during the tribulation.

We are now living in a 2,000 year GAP between the 69th and the 70th week, called the *"Times of the Gentiles"* But this time is about to end, then the tribulation period will begin. Daniel's prophecy tells us of some of the things the antichrist will do. But remember that it is the Church's presence that keeps all of these things from occurring.

Scripture calls this _ruler_ *"the prince who is to come."*
He will confirm a covenant with Israel for one 'seven year period. But in the middle of the 'seven years,' He will set up an abomination that causes desolation in the temple.

Jesus prophesied this event in:
Matthew 24:15
"Therefore when you see the abomination of desolation,' spoken of by Daniel the prophet, standing in the holy place (whoever reads, let him understand)"

Let's examine the Temple:
The Temple Mount consisted of
1. The Outer Court- where Jews and Gentiles could gather.
2. Balustrades (This was a Wall of Separation) which no Gentile could go beyond.

3. Then there was a Court for the Women
4. Then the Court for the Men
5. Then the Holy Place for all the Priests
6. Then the Holy of Holies for the High
   Priest, who would enter into once a year.

John is told to only measure the Temple! "_Naos_" referring to the Temple area distinct from the whole complex. The "Temple" represents Israel's religion, that the Jews will build a Tribulation.

It is believed that when the anti-Christ comes, he will devise a plan that will please both Jews and Arabs. This may happen the way I'm about to show you!

A Balustrade could be built separating what many believe to be the original site of the Holy of Holies from the rest of the complex. Remember the purpose of this wall was to separate the Gentiles from the Jews. It will separate the Naos from the rest of the Hieron.

Principle: Religion blinds people to the truth.

Application: The Great Tribulation will experience the greatest period of religion and satanic worship that the world has ever seen. Religion has forever been a blinder to the truth. Satan will use religion as the basis for his counter revival. Rome will have a world dictator who will be in charge of a world-wide ecumenical religion during the tribulation.

Ecumenicalism: Is a universal unification of Churches that brings in all kinds of different beliefs. When you hear this word, stay away from it.

Let's return to our first two verses, the end of the book of Ezekiel is similar to **_Revelation 11:1-2._**
In **_Ezekiel 40_** the prophet is taken to a high mountain from where he can observe events in Jerusalem. There he meets an angel (a man with the appearance of bronze) with a measuring rod in his hands.

Chapters 40-48 describe Ezekiel measuring the city and the temple area. After the measuring is complete, the glory of the Lord then returns to the temple. Ezekiel's ministry was meant to describe the departure of the glory of the Lord from the temple at the time of the fall of Jerusalem in 586 B. C. and the return of God's glory at the time of the establishment of the kingdom. Maybe John was being directed to do something similar to what

Ezekiel did, indicating the return of the glory of the Lord at the end of Revelation.

The Two Witnesses;
Revelation 11: 4-6

"These are the two olive trees and the two lamp-stands standing before the God of the earth. And if anyone wants to harm them, fire proceeds from their mouth and devours their enemies. And if anyone wants to harm them, he must be killed in this manner. These have power to shut heaven, so that no rain falls in the days of their prophecy; and they have power over waters to turn them to blood, and to strike the earth with all plagues, as often as they desire."

These olive trees and lamp-stand: take us back to the book of **Zechariah 4**, as he prophesies of the restoration of the temple and how the mountain of rubble that was left in the destruction by the Babylonians will be moved *"Not by might or by power but by My Spirit says the Lord of hosts."*

In Zechariah's vision, he sees two olive trees feeding the lampstand, they represent the abundant supply of oil from the Holy Spirit's power which would help Zerubbabel finish rebuilding the temple (symbolized by the large lamp-stand).

The light from the lamp-stand signified that Israel, God's covenant people were to shine forth light and glorify God on the earth. The two olive trees represent Zerubbabel and Joshua, the governor and high priest.

The Lord encourages them not to trust in financial or military resources, but in the power of God's Holy Spirit working through them (**_verse 6_**).

In the last days, the two-witnesses are compared to these Olive trees: Why are they compared to them? Let's begin with the Greek word for witness; it comes from the word martyr. These two words are synonymous. So they will be killed for doing just that "witnessing."
The reason they are compared to olive trees is because they will produce God's light in this time of great darkness. But eventually they will be killed.

Revelation 11: 7-10
"When they finish their testimony, the beast that ascends out of the bottomless pit will make war against them, overcome them, and kill them. And their dead bodies will lie in the street of the Great city which spiritually is called Sodom and Egypt, where also our Lord was

crucified. Then those from the peoples, tribes, tongues, and nations will see their dead bodies three-and-a-half days, and not allow their dead bodies to be put into graves. And those who dwell on the earth will rejoice over them, make merry, and send gifts to one another, because these two prophets tormented those who dwell on the earth."

Who are these two witnesses? We know that one of them will be the prophet Elijah, from Malachi's prophecy stating that he would return before the great day of the Lord.

Malachi 4:5
"Behold, I will send you Elijah the prophet before the coming of the great and dreadful day of the LORD."

But who is the other witness?
Many have speculated that it could be:
1. Moses- because of the similarities in the plagues, and because he represents the law.
2. Enoch- because he didn't die, but many won't die either in the Rapture.
3. John the Baptist - Because of his direct way of speaking and dealing with issues.
4. I guess we will all find out who it will be then!

Now these two witnesses are not killed until, *"They finish their (mission) testimony."* I believe that you and I are also invincible until we finish our earthly assignment, that's why we must keep fulfilling what we've been called to do.

The Beast will rise up against them and kill them. But it is peculiar to note that they were invincible until they finished their assignment. This passage mentions the great city where they will be killed.

Where is this great city?

It is none other than Jerusalem! *"Then those who dwell on the earth will rejoice over them,"* The world will actually celebrate their deaths, because they had become public enemies number one.

Remember that they had *"power to shut heaven, so that no rain falls in the days of their prophecy; and they have power over waters to turn them to blood, and to strike the earth with all plagues, as often as they desire."* But God is not through with these two, quite yet!

The witnesses will be resurrected!

Revelation 11:11-13

"Now after the three-and-a-half days the breath of life from God entered them, and they stood on their feet, and great fear fell on those who saw them. And they heard a loud voice from heaven saying to them, "Come up here." And they ascended to heaven in a cloud, and their enemies saw them. In the same hour there was a great earthquake, and a tenth of the city fell. In the earthquake seven thousand people were killed, and the rest were afraid and gave glory to the God of heaven."

Suddenly in the midst of the world's celebration, God who speaks those things that are not as if though they were, calls these men from the dead to get up and go home to Heaven. Can you just imagine what every secular news media like CNN, ABC, NBC, CBS, is going to report. I believe that the fear of God will fall upon many who had previously not cared for their message. SCRIPTURE SAYS THAT ALL NATIONS, PEOPLE, AND TRIBES WILL SEE THEIR BODIES. With our telecommunication systems covering the entire world there is no doubt that this will happen.

Revelation 11: 14

"The second woe is past. Behold, the third woe is coming quickly."

Seventh Trumpet: The Kingdom is Proclaimed and Worship Breaks out in Heaven.

Revelation 11: 15-19

"Then the seventh angel sounded: And there were loud voices in heaven, saying, "The kingdoms of this world have become the kingdoms of our Lord and of His Christ, and He shall reign forever and ever!" And the twenty-four elders who sat before God on their thrones fell on their faces and worshiped God, saying: "We give You thanks, O Lord God Almighty, the One who is and who was and who is to come, because You have taken Your great power and reigned. The nations were angry, and Your wrath has come, and the time of the dead, that they should be judged, and that You should reward Your servants the prophets and the saints, and those who fear Your name, small and great, and should destroy those who destroy the earth."
Then the temple of God was opened in heaven, and the ark of His covenant was seen in His temple. And there were lightnings, noises, thunderings, an earthquake and great hail."

Jesus will then take complete possession of what is His, (the world) only after all the seals are broken and fulfilled.

Revelation 11:18

"And the time of the dead, that they should be judged, And that You should reward Your servants the prophets and the saints,"

This passage refers to the _Great White Throne Judgment_ that we will talk more about later, when we get there.

Revelation 11: 18

"And those who fear Your name, small and great, and should destroy those who destroy the earth."

This is probably a reference to _Christ 2nd advent_ in:

Revelation 19: 14-15

"And the _armies in heaven,_ clothed in fine linen, white and clean, followed Him on white horses. Now out of His mouth goes a sharp sword, that with it He should strike the nations. And He Himself will rule them with a rod of iron. He Himself treads the winepress of the fierceness and wrath of Almighty God"

Revelation 11:19

"Then the temple of God was opened in heaven, and the ark of His covenant was seen in His temple. And there were lightnings, noises, thunderings, an earthquake, and great hail."

This passage expresses the importance of why God instructed Moses how to build the Tabernacle in the first place. He wanted to dwell among His people on Earth; the earthly tabernacle represents His dwelling place, the heavenly temple.

Now, the Temple of God in Jerusalem was destroyed in AD 70 by the Romans. But when God commanded Moses to build the Temple in the Old Testament, He told him to build it to the specifications he was given because it would be a copy of the Temple in heaven.

Now there is a heavenly sanctuary awaiting us:

Hebrews 9:11
"But Christ came as High Priest of the good things to come, with the greater and more perfect tabernacle not made with hands, that is, not of this creation."

LET US LOOK FORWARD TO THAT!
That's the Temple John is speaking about.

We continue on our quest to understand the prophetic message of Revelation and its significance to an unbelieving world.

"The Woman, the Child and the Dragon"
Chapters 12

Rev. 12:1-2
"Now a great sign appeared in heaven: a woman clothed with the sun, with the moon under her feet, and on her head a garland of twelve stars. Then being with child, she cried out in labor and in pain to give birth."

Who is this woman? Many have mistaken the woman to be Mary or the Church, but that is not so. The woman is none other than Israel. We know this, because of the description given, "The sun, moon under her feet, and a garland of stars on her head. To best understand who she is, let's look in the book of Genesis. When Joseph, Jacob's son had a second dream and he shared it with his family, that even his father became angry with what Joseph was implying.

Genesis 37: 9-10
"Then he dreamed still another dream and told it to his brothers, and said, "Look, I have dreamed another dream. And this time, the sun, the moon, and the eleven stars bowed down to me. So he told it to his father and his brothers; and his father rebuked him and said to him,

"What is this dream that you have dreamed? Shall your mother and I and your brothers indeed come to bow down to the earth before you?"

If you remember, Jacob's name became Israel and so the name of the Nation also became Israel.
Who is this Child?
There are those who argue that the child is Jesus, but this event must be interpreted as occurring during the tribulation.
We must remember that Jesus is already at the right hand of the Father. There is only one group that can fit that identity; it would be those believers (first-fruits) from Israel escaping persecution. The child represents the redeemed of Israel.

Why is Israel being persecuted? Israel has always been persecuted. The reason for their persecution here is because of Jesus, He would bring redemption to the world. Satan tried to enslave and destroy the Jews from the beginning in Egypt with Pharaoh, and then again under Persian rule in the book of Esther. He also attempted to keep Jesus from going to the cross when he tempted Him in the wilderness, offering Jesus the world's kingdoms without having to go to the cross. Why?

Because it was the shed blood of Jesus that would redeem us.

Who is the dragon? Again we find that scripture is the best interpreter of scripture.

Revelation 12:9
"So the great dragon was cast out, that serpent of old, called the Devil and Satan, who deceives the whole world; he was cast to the earth, and his angels were cast out with him."

John again uses metaphorical language to describe satan. Pop culture today, portrays satan red with two horns and a pitch fork. But in reality that is the description of the Greek and Roman god, Pan.

Ezekiel gives us the Biblical description. He was a beautiful creature.

Ezekiel 28:14-15
"You were the anointed cherub who covers; I established you; you were on the holy mountain of God; You walked back and forth in the midst of fiery stones. You were perfect in your ways from the day you were created, till iniquity was found in you."

He was an anointed Cherub.

Revelation 12: 3-6
"And another sign appeared in heaven: behold, a great, fiery red dragon having seven heads and ten horns, and seven diadems on his heads. His tail drew a third of the stars of heaven and threw them to the earth. And the dragon stood before the woman who was ready to give birth, to devour her Child as soon as it was born. She bore a male Child who was to rule all nations with a rod of iron. And her Child was caught up to God and His throne. Then the woman fled into the wilderness, where she has a place prepared by God that they should feed her there one thousand two hundred and sixty days.

Where did the Woman and Child Flee? To Jordan, possibly into the area of Petra, Sela (rock or stronghold) mentioned in **Isaiah 16: 1-5**. Petra is located in the nation of Jordan, just east of Israel where she will escape for the 2nd half of the tribulation, (3 1/2 years.)

God speaks to Israel:
Isaiah 26:20-21
"Come, my people, enter your chambers, And shut your doors behind you;
Hide yourself, as it were, for a little moment, until the indignation is past.

For behold, the LORD comes out of His place to punish the inhabitants of the earth for their iniquity; the earth will also disclose her blood, and will no more cover her slain."

<u>Revelation 12:7-9</u>
"And war broke out in heaven: Michael and his angels fought with the dragon; and the dragon and his angels fought, but they did not prevail, nor was a place found for them in heaven any longer. So the great dragon was cast out, that serpent of old, called the Devil (Accuser) and Satan, (Opposer) who deceives the whole world; he was cast to the earth, and his angels were cast out with him."

It appears from this passage that Micheal and satan (the Dragon) have had a long history of battles, from before time ever was, when satan was cast out of Heaven, again when they disputed over Moses' body. (**<u>Jude 1:9</u>**) When Daniel's prayer was hindered (**<u>Dan. 10:13</u>**) And now we see them fighting in Heaven, satan will be cast down to earth, no longer being permitted access to the third heaven to God's throne *"yet still being able to accuse the brethren."* Angry because he knows that his time is running out. It is important to know that satan is not God's equal.

No created being can ever be!

The Book of Daniel tells of this Battle.

Daniel 12:1
"At that time Michael shall stand up, the great prince who stands watch over the sons of your people; and there shall be a time of trouble, such as never was since there was a nation, Even to that time. and at that time your people shall be delivered, everyone who is found written in the book."

Revelation 12: 10-11
"Then I heard a loud voice saying in heaven, "Now salvation, and strength, and the kingdom of our God, and the power of His Christ have come, for the accuser (satan) of our brethren, who accused them before our God day and night, has been cast down. And they overcame him by the blood of the Lamb and by the word of their testimony, and they did not love their lives to the death."

Let's examine and see what *Revelation 12:11* is saying,
It gives us the key as to how the tribulation saints will overcome the enemy.

1. And they overcame him by blood of the Lamb because there is power in the shed blood of Christ.

Ephesians 1:7
"In Him we have redemption through His blood, the forgiveness of sins, according to the riches of His grace"

Hebrews 9:22
"And according to the law almost all things are purified with blood, and without shedding of blood there is no remission."

2. And the word of their testimony- it is imperative that we live our lives in Active Faith, and protect our name as believers, because our testimony has great power as long as it is credible. But when we fail to keep our commitment to God, It isn't.

We become stumbling blocks at the entry of Gods Kingdom. The life we live and the words we speak are so important, let us always lift the name and the work of Jesus on high.

3. They did not love their lives to the death. - These people will know that God owns them. They did not belong to

themselves any longer. Their mindset will be if we live we serve God; if we die we go to be with Him.

May we understand and live our lives in the reality of this passage!

Revelation 12:12
"Therefore rejoice O heavens, and you who dwell in them! Woe to the inhabitants of the earth and the sea! For the devil has come down to you, having great wrath, because he knows that he has a short time."

It will be during the end of the Tribulation that satan will be cast down to earth, no longer having access to Heaven. So he will unleash much more of his persecution, angered because he knows he only has a little time to do his work.

The Woman Persecuted

Revelation 12:13-17

"Now when the dragon saw that he had been cast to the earth, he persecuted the woman who gave birth to the male Child. But the woman was given two wings of a great eagle that she might fly into the wilderness to her place, where she is nourished for a time and times and half a time from the presence of the serpent. So the serpent spewed water out of his mouth like a flood after the woman, that he might cause her to be carried away by the flood. But the earth helped the woman, and the earth opened its mouth and swallowed up the flood which the dragon had spewed out of his mouth. And the dragon was enraged with the woman, and he went to make war with the rest of her offspring, who keep the commandments of God and have the testimony of Jesus Christ."

This passage depicts the dragon (satan) pursuing Israel in an all-out attempt to destroy her. So he sends out an army to devour her, but to no avail. God protects Israel as she flees into the wilderness, where He sustains her for the second half of the tribulation.
Scripture says for a time (1 Year) and times (2 Years) and half a time, (1/2 year). As Israel runs

into the desert, the serpent spewed water out of his mouth like a flood after the woman, but God commands the Earth to take care of her! Just as he did in the Old Testament.

Remember when Korah led a rebellion against Moses and Aaron, as they questioned their leadership.

Korah said,
"We are all the same as you two, who made you leaders?"
So God had to show them by using the Earth to prove His choice of Authority, in Moses and Aaron.

Numbers 16:3
"They gathered together against Moses and Aaron, and said to them, "You take too much upon yourselves, for all the congregation is holy, every one of them, and the LORD is among them. Why then do you exalt yourselves above the assembly of the LORD?"

Numbers 16: 32-34
"Now it came to pass, as he finished speaking all these words, that the earth opened its mouth and swallowed them up, with their households and all the men with Korah, with all their goods. So they and all those with them went down alive

into the pit; the earth closed over them, and they perished from among the assembly. Then all Israel who were around them fled at their cry, for they said, "Lest the earth swallow us up also!"

True leadership will always be vindicated by God !
As I have mentioned already, the prophet Isaiah revealed the place that God has prepared for Israel to escape during this time. That place is in Edom.

Isaiah 16: 1-5
"Send the lamb to the ruler of the land from Sela to the wilderness, to the mount of the daughter of Zion. For it shall be as a wandering bird thrown out of the nest; so shall be the daughters of Moab at the fords of the Arnon. "Take counsel, execute judgment; Make your shadow like the night in the middle of the day; Hide the outcasts, do not betray him who escapes. Let My outcasts dwell with you, O Moab; Be a shelter to them from the face of the spoiler for the extortioner is at an end, devastation ceases, the oppressors are consumed out of the land. In mercy the throne will be established; and One will sit on it in truth, in the tabernacle of David, judging and seeking justice and hastening righteousness."

Petra is naturally fortified, it is called Sela, (Rock or Stronghold) it was also called Bozrah in **_Amos 1:12_**. Israel's stay there will be for 3 1/2 years, or the last half of the tribulation.

It will be then that Israel will pray for God to come down.

Isaiah 64:1
"Oh, that You would rend the heavens! That You would come down. That the mountains might shake at Your presence"

Two Beasts and Three Angels
Chapter 13

Revelation 13:1-2. The Beast from the Sea.
*"Then I stood on the sand of the sea. And I saw
a beast rising up out of the sea, having seven
heads and ten horns, and on his horns ten
crowns, and on his heads a blasphemous
name. Now the beast which I saw was like
a leopard, his feet were like the feet of a bear,
and his mouth like the mouth of a lion.
The dragon gave him his power, his throne, and
great authority."*

*(Notice that the Dragon will have crowns on his
heads and the Beast will have them on his
horns)*

In this passage, there is a Beast that appears to
be coming out of the sand of the sea,
In the Bible, the sea represents the nations, the
great sea of humanity in the world. There's a
passage in Daniel that will help us better
understand these two verses.

Daniel 7: 2-8
*"Daniel spoke, saying, "I saw in my vision by
night, and behold, the four winds of heaven were
stirring up the Great Sea. And four great
beasts came up from the sea, each different from*

the other. The first was like a lion, (Babylonian Empire) and had eagle's wings. I watched till its wings were plucked off; and it was lifted up from the earth and made to stand on two feet like a man, and a man's heart was given to it. (This was Nebuchadnezzar's story of pride) "And suddenly another beast, a second, like a bear. (Medo Persian Empire) It was raised up on one side and had three ribs in its mouth between its teeth. And they said thus to it: 'Arise, devour much flesh!' "After this I looked, and there was another, like a leopard, (Greek Empire) which had on its back four wings of a bird. The beast also had four heads, and dominion was given to it. "After this I saw in the night visions, and behold, a fourth beast, (This non-discript Beast represents the Roman Empire) dreadful and terrible, exceedingly strong. It had huge iron teeth; it was devouring, breaking in pieces, and trampling the residue with its feet. It was different from all the beasts that were before it, and it had ten horns. I was considering the horns, and there was another horn, a little one, coming up among them, before whom three of the first horns were plucked out by the roots. And there, in this horn, were eyes like the eyes of a man, and a mouth speaking pompous words."

This little horn coming out of the ten horns, is the Beast in **_Rev. 13:1-2_**. The 4 Beasts in

Daniel's Vision are empires that have existed and ruled the world in their time.
1. Babylon
2. Medo-Persia
3. Greek
4. Roman

Although John lived during the fourth kingdom, Rome was never really defeated, it just seemed to have fallen apart. Daniel sees a confederation of nations, rising out of the Old Roman Empire.

According to _Dan. 7: 24:_
"The ten horns are ten kings who shall arise from this kingdom. and another shall rise after them; He shall be different from the first ones and shall subdue three kings."

In Daniel's Vision, he also sees "The little horn" that will come forth out of the 10 Nation Confederation. He will pluck out three leaving only 7 horns.

This Beast is the anti-Christ (little horn) the imitation of Jesus, who will attempt to take His place. He is the little horn of _**Daniel 7:8**_. The Man of Sin and the Man of Perdition, _**2 Thess. 2:3**_. The anti-Christ will not come forth until the church is removed/raptured from the world.

The seven heads (Beast) are the 7 Mountains upon which the woman (Great Harlot- Spiritual Babylon sits) explained in:
Revelation 17:9: *"Here is the mind which has wisdom: The seven heads are seven mountains on which the woman sits."*
Rome is built on 7 hills/mountains. And this could also signify that Rome might be the seat of his Authority.

Daniel 7-8 record the vision of these 4 kingdoms.

Then in Chapter 9, as Daniel is praying for the people, confessing, and repenting of their sin. Understanding that their 70 years of slavery was about up.
God gives him another Vision. Dealing with Israel, Daniel's 70 weeks of 7 years, a total of 490 years. The purpose for this time period is explained in **_Daniel 9: 20-27_**. The Angel Gabriel explains to Daniel the 70 week vision to him.

Daniel 9:24
"Seventy weeks are determined for your people and for your holy city, To finish the

transgression, to make an end of sins, to make reconciliation for iniquity, to bring in everlasting righteousness, to seal up vision and prophecy, and to anoint the Most Holy."

Then the Angel continues to explain that from the time that Cyrus' decree would go out, to the time that Jesus would enter Jerusalem would be a span of 483 years. That still leaves a 7 year period of time when God will continue to deal with Israel, still unaccounted for.

Gabriel continues to explain:
Daniel 9:26
"And after the sixty-two weeks Messiah shall be cut off, but not for Himself; and the people scattered."

True to the scripture Jesus was crucified. From the end of the 62 weeks until now, we have been living in a gap of time Jesus calls the _Times of the Gentiles._

Luke 21:24
"And they will fall by the edge of the sword, and be led away captive into all nations. And Jerusalem will be trampled by Gentiles until the times of the Gentiles are fulfilled."

We know it better as the _Dispensation of Grace_. But we are now at the end of the times of the Gentiles. The signs of the times are everywhere. The tribulation period will soon become reality. It will be the last 7 years that God deals with Israel.

As I mentioned before, there will be a great upsurge of religion to take place in the last days, because religion blinds people to the truth. Scripture reveals this!
Listen to these words, There will come a time when the antichrist will be mortally wounded.

Revelation 13: 3-4
"The dragon gave him his power, his throne, and great authority. And I saw one of his heads as if it had been mortally wounded, and his deadly wound was healed.
And all the world marveled and followed the beast. So they (worshiped the dragon) who gave authority to the beast; and they worshiped the beast, saying, Who is like the beast? Who is able to make war with him?"

Because of these satanic type miracles worship of Satan will become popular. Satan will also give this beast the power and authority that Adam gave him in the garden. "Who is like the

beast? (anti-Christ) His abilities will be far beyond normal human ones.
Who is able to make war with him?"

Revelation 13: 5-6 The Anti-Christ
"And he was given a mouth speaking great things and blasphemies, and he was given authority to continue for forty-two months. Then he opened his mouth in blasphemy against God, to blaspheme His name, His tabernacle, and those who dwell in heaven."

Then he opened his mouth in blasphemy against God, to blaspheme His name, His tabernacle, and those who dwell in heaven"

We can see the great power that words have, whosever they are! Good or Bad words, they matter! So we must be thoughtful and careful what we speak and what we listen to.

Revelation 13: 7-10
"It was granted to him to make war with the saints and to overcome them."
(Remember, these will be believers from Israel and others coming forth out of the tribulation. At this time the Church will already be in heaven)
And authority was given him over every tribe, tongue, and nation. All who dwell on the earth

will worship him, whose names have not been written in the Book of Life of the Lamb slain from the foundation of the world. If anyone has an ear, let him hear. He who leads into captivity shall go into captivity; he who kills with the sword must be killed with the sword. Here is the patience and the faith of the saints"

Then a second Beast will come out of from the Earth.

Revelation 13:11-18

"Then I saw another beast (This is the False Prophet) coming up out of the earth, and he had two horns like a lamb and spoke like a dragon. And he exercises all the authority of the first beast in his presence, and causes the earth and those who dwell in it to worship the first beast, whose deadly wound was healed. He performs great signs, so that he even makes fire come down from heaven on the earth in the sight of men.
And he deceives those who dwell on the earth by those signs which he was granted to do in the sight of the beast, telling those who dwell on the earth to make an image to the beast who was wounded by the sword and lived. He was granted power to give breath to the image of the beast, that the image of the beast should both speak and cause as many as would not worship the image of the beast to be killed. He causes all,

both small and great, rich and poor, free and slave, to receive a mark on their right hand or on their foreheads, and that no one may buy or sell except one who has the mark or the name of the beast, or the number of his name. Here is wisdom. Let him who has understanding calculate the number of the beast, for it is the number of a man: His number is 666."

What do the two horns on this 2nd beast represent?
These are the deceptive signs of the peaceful like qualities of a Lamb that he will present to the world, making him acceptable.

This second beast (false Prophet) will be a false Imitation of the Holy Spirit; he will perform miracles and lying wonders to deceive the world.

You and I then must be careful
1. To discern and recognize the real from
             the fabricated,
2. The original from a copy,
3. The genuine from a fake.

In order that the world worship and adore the anti Christ, the false prophet will use his powers of persuasion. His humble appearance will be deceptively harmless.

But ultimately he becomes destructive. He will share authority with the first beast. (anti-Christ) His assignment will be to cause everyone to worship the first beast. He will demand that everyone receive the mark of the beast on their forehead or right hand

(v.:16–17).
Here we get a glimpse of the satanic trinity at work!
1. Dragon
2. False Prophet
3. Anti- Christ

What is the image of the beast? The false prophet will cause the world to build an image of the beast, giving it life and demanding the world to worship it. The false prophet will perform great miracles giving the anti-Christ credibility. He will also deceive many causing people to worship the 1st beast causing many to receive the mark of the beast.

What does the number 666 symbolize? The Mark of the beast will act as a seal for the followers of the anti-Christ and the false prophet. It will literally be placed on the hand or forehead; it won't be simply a card someone carries.

The recent breakthroughs in medical chip implant and RFID technologies. (Radio Frequency Identification) is used to identify and track people or objects. This technology has increased interest in the mark of the beast. It is possible that the technology we are seeing today represents the beginning stages of what may eventually be used as the mark of the beast.

Some expositors say, it is important to realize that a medical chip implant is not the mark of the beast. The mark of the beast will be an end-time identification required by the anti-Christ in order to buy or sell; it will be given only to those who worship the anti-Christ. It seems to me that this technology could be later used for those evil purposes.

The Earth's Harvest
Chapters 14

These *chapters* tell the story of:
1. The Lamb and the *144,000 witnesses*
2. The *three angel's messages*
3. A *voice* coming from heaven,
4. The tribulation *harvest*

The 144,000 witnesses *announce* the arrival of *God's final judgment hour, they proclaim* salvation through Christ, and announce His second coming. This proclamation is made by the three angels in Revelation 14.

Revelations 14: Throughout this revelation experience, John is a spectator.
Rev. 14:1
"Then I looked, and behold, a Lamb standing on Mount Zion, and with Him one hundred and forty-four thousand, having His Father's name written on their foreheads."

This passage deals with the 144,000 Jewish witnesses God will raise out of Israel, Jews who will be saved!

In Revelation 7,

When the four Angels were about to release the devastating winds on to the earth they were told to wait, Until all of the children of God were sealed on their foreheads,

Now, here we are told what that seal was, His Father's name will be written on their foreheads. (His name as Jehova or Yahweh,). It is interesting to note that the anti-Christ will also want to place his mark/name on his followers his followers foreheads during the great tribulation. In the Hebrew alphabet every letter has a number value. His mark will be the number of his name.

Revelation 14:2-3

"And I heard a voice from heaven, like the voice of many waters, and like the voice of loud thunder."

God's Voice in scripture has been compared to:
1. Thunder
2. Rushing Waters
3. A still small voice

I believe He allows it to be heard according to the need of the moment.

"And I heard the sound of harpists playing their harps. They sang as it were a New Song before the throne, before the four living creatures, and the elders; and no one could learn that song except the hundred and forty-four thousand who were redeemed from the earth."

Note: It appears that every group mentioned in the bible has their own song to sing; in this passage we see the 144,000 singing their song.

In the Old Testament:
1. We see the Song of Moses in ***Ex. 15***. Moses and Israel had a song of deliverance to sing, as they emerged out of the Red Sea; leaving Egypt, Pharaoh and Slavery behind them.

2. The Song of Deborah, ***Judges 5*** (They sang a song of victory over their enemy).
Deborah was the only woman judge over Israel during the time of the Judges. She was called to be a wife, a prophetess, and a judge over Israel. She led her nation to victory, when men were afraid to go out and face the enemy.

In The New Testament in Revelation 5, we find the Song of the Church. It is a Song of Redemption and of Deliverance from the Great Tribulation, that only we will sing.

The 144,000 will have their own song that only they will be able to sing, but their song is one of preservation through the great tribulation.

It seems that each group will be able to relate to God in their own special way.

Revelation 14:4-5 *Description of the 144,000 "These are the ones who were not defiled with women, for they are virgins.*
These are the ones who follow the lamb wherever He goes. These were redeemed from among men, being first fruits to God and to the Lamb and in their mouth was found no deceit, for they are without fault before the throne of God."

Note*:* -The 144,000 are converted Jewish evangelists sent out to bring sinners to Jesus Christ during the seven year tribulation period. These are the first fruits of a special order, they will be without fault or deceit. In fact that is how we will all stand before the Lord!

Jude 1:24
"Now to Him who is able to keep you from stumbling and <u>to present you faultless</u> before the presence of His glory with exceeding joy,"

What's amazing is that, this is the how <u>God sees you and I, Now!</u>

Then John saw another angel!
Revelation 14: 6-7,
"Then I saw another angel flying in the midst of heaven, having the everlasting gospel to preach to those who dwell on the earth—to every nation, tribe, tongue, and people—saying with a loud voice, "Fear God and give glory to Him, for the hour of His judgment has come; and worship Him who made heaven and earth, the sea and springs of water."

The whole world will be able to see this angel in real time. Through our modern telecommunication's systems. This angel's message will call people to the:
1. Fear of God
2. To give Him Glory
3. To worship Him because the hour of God's Judgment has come.

Revelation 14: 8 *A second angel*
"And another angel followed, saying, "Babylon is fallen, is fallen, that great city, because she has made all nations drink of the wine of the wrath of her fornication."

Who is this Babylon? We will encounter who she is, in **_Revelation 17_** when we read of God's judgment of religious Babylon.
And then of His judgment of commercial Babylon in **_Rev. 18._** Here we see the pronouncement of these things.

What is this Wine of Wrath?
It is the participation or partaking in false religious systems - (called fornication). From the worship of Semiramis and her child Tammuz, (in Assyria), who in time became her husband. To the worship of Mary today. Religion has a way of masking, or obscuring God's truth. Satan will use religion greatly in the tribulation.

Revelation 14: 9-10, *A Third Angel*
"And then a third angel followed them, saying with a loud voice, "If anyone worships the beast and his image, and receives his mark on his forehead or on his hand, he himself shall also drink of the wine of the wrath of God, which is poured out full strength into the cup of His

indignation. He shall be tormented with fire and brimstone in the presence of the holy angels and in the presence of the Lamb."

<u>**Note**</u>*:* Here, God gives those who would think of worshipping the beast or taking his mark as a warning. There will be no hope of redemption, salvation, or mercy for those who worship and receive the Mark of the Beast. They will have signed their own Death Certificate; they will be tormented in the presence of God's holy angels and the Lamb. This is something that bothers many believers who are concerned about their family members who have died and were not saved who will be tortured and separated from God throughout eternity. What will that saved loved one feel for them then? How can we ever enjoy Heaven with the thoughts of a loved one being tortured?

Isaiah gives us an answer to that.
Isaiah 65:17
"For behold, I create new heavens and a new earth; and the former shall not be remembered or come to mind."

Anything or thought that would bring you pain or torture will be removed from your consciousness.

Isaiah 65:18-19

"But be glad and rejoice forever in what I create; for behold, I create Jerusalem as a rejoicing, and her people a joy. I will rejoice in Jerusalem, and joy in My people;
The voice of weeping shall no longer be heard in her, nor the voice of crying.......
It shall come to pass that before they call, I will answer; and while they are still speaking, I will hear. The wolf and the lamb shall feed together, the lion shall eat straw like the ox, and dust shall be the serpent's food. They shall not hurt nor destroy in all my holy mountain," says the LORD."

This is what awaits God's elect! But for those who choose not to receive Christ, and live their lives without him, this is what awaits them:

Revelation 14: 11

"And the smoke of their torment ascends forever and ever; (Eternity) and they have no rest day or night, who worship the beast and his image, and whoever receives the mark (666) of his name."

Revelation 13: 17-18

"And that no one may buy or sell except one who has the mark or the name of the beast, or the number of his name. Wisdom is needed here. Let the one with understanding solve the

meaning of the number of the beast, for it is the number of a man. His number is 666."

<u>Gematria:</u> This word is of Hebrew origin, it is an ancient method of assigning a numerical value to each letter of a word, name, or expression to figure the hidden meaning of the word.

<u>Rev. 14:9,</u> tells us that any worship other than to God is <u>spiritual fornication</u>. Here is a warning against it. You don't want to wind up tormented in <u>Gehenna</u> (Hell).

<u>Jesus warns us:</u>
<u>Mark 9: 43-44</u>
"If your hand causes you to sin, cut it off. It is better for you to enter into life maimed, rather than having two hands, to go to hell, into the fire that shall never be quenched— where their <u>worm</u> does not die and the fire is not quenched"

<u>Rev. 14: 12- 13,</u>
"Here is the patience of the saints; here are those who keep the commandments of God and the faith of Jesus.
Then I heard a voice from heaven saying to me, write: Blessed are the dead who die in the Lord from now on.' "Yes," says the Spirit: "that they

may rest from their labors, and their works follow them."

This is the patience and faithfulness of those who would rather be martyred than to take the mark. It will be better to die for your faith than to worship the beast or take his mark and end up in Hell. Those who do will have sealed their own fate.

Now we get a glimpse of Armageddon.
Reaping the Earth's Harvest
Revelation 14: 14-16
"Then I looked, and behold, a white cloud, and on the cloud sat One like the Son of Man, having on His head a golden crown, and in His hand a sharp sickle. And another angel came out of the temple, crying with a loud voice to Him who sat on the cloud, Thrust in Your sickle and reap, for the time has come for You to reap, for the harvest of the earth is ripe. So He who sat on the cloud thrust in His sickle on the earth, and the earth was reaped."

This is none other than Jesus our Lord.
Revelation 1:7
"Behold he comes in the clouds to bring judgment upon the earth."

<u>**Revelation 14: 17-20**</u>, *"then another angel came out of the temple which is in heaven, he also having a sharp sickle. And another angel came out from the altar, who had power over fire, and he cried with a loud cry to him who had the sharp sickle, saying, "Thrust in your sharp sickle and gather the clusters of the vine of the earth, for her grapes are fully ripe." So the angel thrust his sickle into the earth and gathered the vine of the earth, and threw it into the great winepress of the wrath of God. And the winepress was trampled outside the city, and blood came out of the winepress, up to the horses' bridles, (4 feet high) for one thousand six hundred furlongs." (That's about 185 miles)*

This is a description of the results of the Battle of Armageddon and all the blood that will be shed there. The Prophet Isaiah speaks of this very battle and its results, here's the description;

<u>**Isaiah 63 1-6**</u>
'Who is this who comes from Edom, With dyed garments from Bozrah,
This One who is glorious in His apparel.
Traveling in the greatness of His strength?—"I who speak in righteousness, mighty to save."
Why is Your apparel red, And Your garments like one who treads in the winepress? "I have

trodden the winepress alone, and from the peoples no one was with Me. For I have trodden them in My anger, And trampled them in My fury; Their blood is sprinkled upon My garments, And I have stained all My robes. For the day of vengeance is in My heart, And the year of My redeemed has come. I looked, but there was no one to help, And I wondered that there was no one to uphold; therefore My own arm brought salvation for Me; And My own fury, it sustained Me. I have trodden down the peoples in My anger, made them drunk in My fury, and brought down their strength to the earth."

Armageddon will be the attempt of the anti-Christ to raise up forces against the Lord, but they will be slaughtered. This will occur the moment that Jesus returns to establish His Kingdom upon the Earth.

<u>Zechariah 14:4</u>
"And in that day His feet will stand on the Mount of Olives, which faces Jerusalem on the east. And the Mount of Olives shall be split in two, from east to west, making a very large valley; half of the mountain shall move toward the north and half of it toward the south."

We are told in _Revelation 19,_
"That he will destroy the anti-Christ and his forces, by the brightness of His coming and by the Sword that comes forth from His mouth, with His Word alone!"

These things are coming, the judgment of God's will must come as He has declared it!

Bowl Judgements and Armageddon
Chapter 15-16

Revelation 15-16; Tells of some of the *last events* that will occur *before the Kingdom Age* and the *devil comes to an end.*

Revelation 15: John sees God's Saints in glory, praising Him *for His righteous judgments,* and the *seven angels* ready to pour out "The Seven last plagues" on the earth (**v. 1**). John continues to speak about the *Battle of Armageddon.*

Revelation 15-16 are both parenthetical chapters.
We must remember that Revelation is not written in a linear form/mode, in other words it's not written in the order it will happen. It is written like Genesis 1 and 2, chapter 1 explains the entire process of Creation, then chapter 2 fills in more information. That's what chapter 15 does. It gives further information on what has already been covered.

Revelation 15:1 Prelude to the bowl judgments
"Then I saw another sign in heaven, great and marvelous: seven angels having the seven last plagues, for in them the wrath of God is complete."

<u>**Note**</u>: These seven angels will be given 7 bowls filled full of God's judgment wrath. At the end of the 7th Bowl this will mark the end of God's tribulation judgment.

<u>The Redeemed will all Sing!</u>
<u>Revelation. 15: 2-4</u>

"And I saw something like a sea of glass mingled with fire, and those who have the victory over the beast, over his image and over his mark and over the number of his name, standing on the sea of glass, having harps of God. They sing the song of Moses, the servant of God, and the song of the Lamb, saying: "Great and marvelous are Your works, Lord God Almighty! Just and true are Your ways, O King of the saints! Who shall not fear You, O Lord, and glorify Your name? For You alone are holy. For all nations shall come and worship before You, for Your judgments have been manifested."

We read about the tribulation saints in **Rev. 7**, these are none other than the martyrs and survivors who got victory over the Beast. Their victory was not in defeating him, but rather in not allowing the beast to defeat them. They will have a song to sing, and this is their song. They sang about how just and true are God's ways. Too often God gets the blame for disastrous things that happen on earth, without realizing that it is satan who controls this world's system today. Paul calls him the *"Prince of the Power of the air"*

Here are people who will be killed because they refused to worship the beast or take his mark. And they don't blame God for it because they understand the score. Theirs's was a self-inflicted wound because they rejected Christ. Often times when people don't understand that their decisions bring consequences and that this world continues to be under satan's power, and bad things happen to them, they are ready to blame God. Here are individuals who don't blame him.

"Who shall not fear You, O Lord, and glorify Your name? For you alone are holy."

<u>Today many don't fear God because they don't really know Him or His plans.</u>
Revelation 15: 5-8
"After these things I looked, and behold, the temple of the tabernacle of the testimony in heaven was opened. And out of the temple came the seven angels having the seven plagues, clothed in pure bright linen, and having their chests girded with golden bands. Then one of the four living creatures gave to the seven angel's seven golden bowls full of the wrath of God who lives forever and ever. The temple was filled with

smoke from the glory of God and from His power, and no one was able to enter the temple till the seven plagues of the seven angels were completed."

There is a tabernacle in Heaven. The one that God commanded Moses to replicate on Earth. If you want to have a glimpse of heaven just look at the tabernacle in the Old Testament.

The tabernacle in the wilderness stood in the middle of Israel's camp. As they traveled through the wilderness there were three tribes to the North, three tribes to the South, three tribes to the East and West. With the Tribe of the Levites divided in three groups immediately around the tabernacle Gershon, Kohath, and Merari: and at the entry was Moses, Aaron and God. God was Israel's focus. God was in their midst continually.
While this fact was true, Israel was undefeatable, so was America at one time in her history.

Let us understand from where we have fallen and place God back in the center of our lives, family and our Nation.

Revelations 16: The 7 bowl judgments
Here we are at another _parenthetical chapter._

John actually begins to introduce chapter 16 in the first verse of chapter 15.

Revelation 15:1
"Then I saw another sign in heaven, great and marvelous: seven angels having the seven last plagues, for in them the wrath of God is complete."

Revelation 16:1 -2 *The first Bowl Judgement*
"Then I heard a loud voice from the temple saying to the seven angels, Go and pour out the bowls of the wrath of God on the earth. So the first went and poured out his bowl upon the earth, and a foul and loathsome sore came upon the men who had the mark of the beast and those who worshiped his image."

These sores are described as very painful, like *foul runny infections that have no cure.* They could be compared to the flesh eating bacteria that people have already contracted. These sores could be caused by high radiation levels brought on by the previous plagues.

Revelation 16:3 Second *Bowl: The sea turns to Blood.*

"Then the second angel poured out his bowl on the sea, and it became blood as of a dead man; and every living creature in the sea died."

*Remember back in **Revelation 8:9** in the trumpet judgments, only one third of the sea turned to blood, but now every ocean and sea will be cursed.*

***Revelation 16:4 -7** Third Bowl: The fresh waters turn to blood*
"Then the third angel poured out his bowl on the rivers and springs of water, and they became blood. And I heard the angel of the waters saying: "You are righteous, O Lord, the One who is and who was and who is to be, because you have judged these things. For they have shed the blood of saints and prophets, and You have given them blood to drink. for it is their just due." And I heard another from the altar saying, "Even so, Lord God Almighty, true and righteous are Your judgments."

The justice system in our nation has many faults and makes many mistakes. But not so God's judgments, His decisions are right on target every-time on every situation.

The angel's comment here refers to the fact that evil people have shed the blood of so many of God's children, that it is fitting that now God will give them blood to drink.

I'm reminded of a story that I read out of Foxes Book of Martyrs from 1999. Graham and Gladys Staines and their two sons felt a call to go India and give medical attention to a Leper Colony. One night after Graham and his sons had ministered to the wounds of these outcasts, cruel men, surrounded the vehicle they were in and began to destroy the car and they beat the father and two little boys. Then they set the station wagon they were sleeping in on fire. All that was left was their charred bodies. We have already seen the blood of martyr spilled.

Revelation 16:8-9 *Fourth Bowl:* *Men are scorched*
"Then the fourth angel poured out his bowl on the sun, and power was given to him to scorch men with fire. And men were scorched with great heat, and they blasphemed the name of God who has power over these plagues; and they did not repent and give Him glory."

How could this happen? Well there are several ways, because the previous plagues will have caused the earth to drift off course and end up closer to the Sun, or there could be a <u>Super Nova</u>,(the Sun becoming hotter than usual.)

We can only be thankful that God is so wise; He has placed earth just close enough to the sun for us to be warm, any further and this planet would be frozen but any closer and it would be burned up.

<u>Rev. 16:10-11 Fifth Bowl</u>*: Darkness and pain* *"Then the fifth angel poured out his bowl on the throne of the beast, and his kingdom became full of darkness; and they gnawed their tongues because of the pain. They blasphemed the God of heaven because of their pains and their sores, and did not repent of their deeds. The sun will be blotted out."*
Can you imagine/perceive the world in complete <u>darkness, cold</u> and in so much pain that it causes complete people to chew their tongues. Yet, instead of repenting their response is that they harden their hearts. You would think that they would have a change of heart and begin to fear God. But they react just the opposite! (Let me share the Illustration of a Knot on a Wet Rope).

When a knot is placed on a wet rope, the tighter you make it, the more of what is in the knot will pour out.

All the <u>rebellion</u> and <u>blasphemy</u> that will be in them will be demonstrated.)

<u>Rev. 16:12-16 Sixth Bowl:</u> The Euphrates Dries Up

"Then the sixth angel poured out his bowl on the great river Euphrates, and its water was dried up, so that the way of the kings from the east might be prepared.
*And I saw three unclean spirits like frogs coming out of the mouth of **the dragon,** out of the mouth of the beast, and out of the mouth of the false prophet. For they are spirits of demons, performing signs, which go out to the kings of the earth and of the whole world, to gather them to the battle of that great day of God Almighty.*
"Behold, I am coming as a thief. Blessed is he who watches, and keeps his garments, lest he walk naked and they see his shame. And they gathered them together to the place called in Hebrew, <u>Armageddon</u>."

<u>Note:</u> The Euphrates River has long been considered in that part of the world as the separation between east and west. In that day it will be dried up so that the leaders who will prepare to fight in the Battle of Armageddon can cross their troops. These frog-like evil spirits that flow from the mouth of each of the

satanic trinity will only serve to further encourage and deceive these leaders to come and do battle against the Lord.

But blessed are those tribulation saints who will not be intimidated or persuaded to change their confession of faith in Christ. But will remain dressed in the righteousness of God in Christ. Just think of how hard it will be to remain faithful to Jesus then, if people find it hard to remain faithful to Him now.

Revelation 16: 17-21 Seventh Bowl: *The earth utterly shaken*
"Then the seventh angel poured out his bowl into the air, and a loud voice came out of the temple of heaven, from the throne, saying, "It is done!" And there were noises and thunderings and lightnings; and there was a Great Earthquake, such, a mighty and great earthquake as had not occurred since men were on the earth. Now the great city (spiritual Babylon) was divided into three parts, and the cities of the nation's fell. And great Babylon was remembered before God, to give her the cup of the wine of the fierceness of His wrath. Then every island fled away, and the mountains were not found. And great hail from heaven fell upon men, each hailstone about the weight of a talent. (A Jewish talent 75 lbs, a Roman talent

129 lbs., just think of the damage that they will do) Men blasphemed God because of the plague of the hail, since that plague was exceedingly great."

Note: What did the Angel mean, "It is done/finished" well from Revelation Chapter 6 on through 18 ; the world has experienced the "Judgments of God."
The bowl judgments are the end of God's wrath poured out on an unrepentant world.

Now, we must take note that the trumpet judgments only destroyed 1/3 of all they touched. But the bowl judgments destroyed everything. So everything is now finished and destroyed.
And again we continue to see that the evil in men's hearts is brought forth as God's judgments become stronger. Yet they are without repentance! Let us pray that we nor our descendants be a part of that group. That we would all serve God faithfully.

The Woman on the Beast
and Fall of Babylon
Chapter 17-18

Revelation 17. *The scarlet woman and the scarlet beast. The judgment and fall of religious Babylon.*

Revelation 17: 1-6
"Then one of the seven angels who had the seven bowls came and talked with me, saying to me, Come, I will show you the judgment of the great harlot who sits on many waters, with whom the kings of the earth committed fornication, and the inhabitants of the earth were made drunk with the wine of her fornication."
So he carried me away in the Spirit into the wilderness. And I saw a woman sitting on a scarlet beast which was full of names of blasphemy, having seven heads and ten horns.
The woman was arrayed in purple and scarlet, and adorned with gold and precious stones and pearls, having in her hand a golden cup full of abominations and the filthiness of her fornication.
And on her forehead a name was written: MYSTERY, BABYLON THE GREAT, THE MOTHER OF HARLOTS AND OF THE ABOMINATIONS OF THE EARTH. I saw

the woman, drunk with the blood of the saints and with the blood of the martyrs of Jesus. And when I saw her, I marveled with great amazement."

Note: Revelation mentions three women,
1. One being this harlot
2. The other being the bride of Christ (**Rev. 21:9-10**)
3. The third being Israel as she flees persecution.

This is the Judgment of God on the false religious system. As always, scripture is the best interpreter of scripture, here it gives us the meaning of the woman and the beast.

Revelation 17:15 (explains the Waters that the Harlot sits on)
"Then the angel said to me, 'The waters you saw, where the prostitute sits, are peoples, multitudes, nations and languages."

The beast mentioned in this verse, is the same beast in **Revelation 13:1,**
"And I saw a beast coming out of the sea. He had ten horns and seven heads, with ten crowns on his horns, and on each head a blasphemous name."

<u>**Note**</u>: This passage refers to the a*nti-Christ*, the man of lawlessness mentioned in
<u>**2 Thessalonians 2: 3-4.**</u>

The whore of Babylon is the religious system in the world, who will be closely affiliated with the antichrist in the end-times.

We can see that the ten horns and seven heads are identified with the revival of the Old Roman Empire, and the Anti-Christ who will come out of that federation of nations.

John saw a woman dressed in Purple and Scarlet, she is called the mother of harlots sitting, upon this scarlet colored beast, full of the names of blasphemy.

So we can see a connection between the anti-Christ and the false religious system.

Who is full of the names of blasphemy?

I've always believed that no one becomes greater or better by tearing others down. But history records these facts that can't be changed, so I'm going to read you some facts written in history out of Halley's Bible Handbook.

The Catholic Church in its history has made some proclamations that stand to this day. Catholicism says that the Pope holds the place of God upon the earth. They have supreme authority over the human conscience that they have power to forgive sin. They have power to grant indulgences and that obedience to them is necessary for Salvation.

The scarlet color of the beast, is the color that the papacy has adopted for all of its cardinals from whom the popes are chosen from. This was originally Satan's color. All of this means that there will be a connection between the false church and the anti-Christ in the tribulation.

Halley's Bible Handbook tells of the murders and prostitution that took place in the history of some of the popes. One Pope, John XII was killed by the woman's husband whom the Pope was having an affair with. Knowing all of this, people are still supposed to believe that this is the office of the men who are supposed to hold the place of God on earth.
So John is writing under the leadership of the Holy Spirit, he tells of this connection that will exist between this false religion and the anti-Christ promoting his actions.

Revelation 17:7-8

"But the angel said to me, "Why did you marvel? I will tell you the mystery of the woman and of the beast that carries her, which has the seven heads and the ten horns." The beast that you saw was, and is not, and will ascend out of the bottomless pit (Abuzo) and go to perdition. And those who dwell on the earth will marvel, whose names are not written in the Book of Life from the foundation of the world, when they see the beast that was, and is not, and yet is."

<u>Note</u>: The whore of Babylon (the religious system) will have great worldwide influence over people and nations.

All of my Christian life, I've been taught that this whore is none other than the Catholic Church. But in the last 20-30 years there's been such a rise of <u>open </u>acceptance and tolerance of false teaching and ungodly lifestyles accepted as part of the protestant mainline church. What I'm saying is that, I don't believe that God is only going to focus on any one religion. But on any and all churches who will not align themselves with what Jesus spoke against in Revelation 2-3, they will all be held accountable also. We must understand that anything that will cause people to turn from worshipping Jesus alone is considered fornication. It is spiritual adultery!

Revelation 17:9-14
"Here is the mind which has wisdom:
The sevenheads are seven mountains on which
the woman sits. "There are also seven kings. Five
have fallen, one is, and the other has not yet
come. And when he comes, he must continue a
short time. The beast that was, and is not, is
himself also the eighth, and is of the seven, and
is going to perdition. "The ten horns which you
saw are ten kings who have received no kingdom
as yet, but they receive authority for one hour as
kings with the beast. These are of one mind, and
they will give their power and authority to the
beast. These will make war with the Lamb, and
the Lamb will overcome them, for He is Lord of
lords and King of kings; and those who are with
Him are called, chosen, and faithful."

<u>Note:</u> These verses describe a series of eight
and then ten kings who will affiliate with the
beast. The whore of Babylon will at one time
have control over these kings, (leaders). This
beast is none other than the anti-Christ.
 Who are these Seven Heads, (Dr. Elizabeth
Williams) in her book "<u>Prevision of History</u>"
writes Seven Heads - gives us an interpretation,
that the 7 heads referred to here are the Kings

and kingdoms which coincide with the "Times of the Gentiles" that have ruled over Israel. Going back into history from John's time. These being: Egypt, Assyria, Babylon, Medo-Persia, Greece and Rome the Empire ruling in John's day. The 7th future empire would be the revived Roman Empire. So the anti-Christ's world empire would be the 7th, and he would be the eighth.

She continues to say, "This interpretation makes plain the wounding and reviving of the head. Imperial Rome was divided as symbolized by the two legs of the metallic man of ***Daniel 2.***

It has laid dormant through the centuries, yet held together by the two legs of Ecclesiastical Christendom, and finds it revived political form in the "Ten Toe Kingdom." It is further seen by Daniel as the "little horn" ruling over the ten kingdoms and becoming the eighth as given by John."

Revelation 17: 15- 18
"Then he said to me, "The waters which you saw, where the harlot sits, are peoples, multitudes, nations, and tongues. And the ten horns which you saw on the beast, these will hate the harlot, make her desolate and naked, eat her flesh and burn her with fire. For God has put it into their hearts to fulfill His purpose, to be of

one mind, and to give their kingdom to the beast, until the words of God are fulfilled. And the woman whom you saw is that great city which reigns over the kings of the earth."

Revelation 18

In our *last* chapter we looked at *God's judgment* on the *false religious system* that will *partner up* with the anti-Christ, but who herself will eventually be disposed of by the *10 nation federation* that will *bring forth* the person that scripture calls the b*east* and the *son of perdition.*

Now, we will look into the destruction of political/material *Babylon* as God prepares the way for the *return of Christ* to officially take *possession of earth*, and of all He purchased at Calvary.

<u>*Revelation 18:1-3*</u> The Fall of political Babylon. *"After these things I saw another angel coming down from heaven, having great authority, and the earth was illuminated with his glory. And he cried mightily with a loud voice, saying, "Babylon the great is fallen, is fallen, and has become a dwelling place of demons, a prison for every foul spirit, and a cage for every unclean and hated bird! For all the nations have drunk of the wine of the wrath of her fornication, the kings of the earth have committed fornication with her, and the merchants of the earth have become rich through the abundance of her luxury."*

<u>**Note**</u>*:* We can easily see the great influence that this Babylonian Spirit has had upon the world throughout history. Although Baylon no longer exists, that Spirit of false religion and of materialism still continues to exist and increase ever so strong.

Now, I want to distinguish between Babylon the false religious system that we looked at in our previous chapter and Babylon the financial system.

We have all been created to be spiritual beings, with an inward yearning for spiritual food. This hunger can only be satisfied as scripture says, *"Blessed are those who hunger and thirst for righteousness sake for they will be satisfied."* (**Matt. 5:6**)
But too often we attempt to satisfy that huger with an emotional moment, relational experiences or by acquiring some material object in our lives.

Let me explain, Companies with their slick advertisements, so easily persuade us to believe that if we just buy their product, that car, watch, ring, home, or those clothes, we will be satisfied. Or if we just have a fling with someone outside of marriage, or some forbidden relationship, or adopt a gay or lesbian lifestyle or maybe attend a particular event, then we will surely be satisfied. But our satisfaction in all of those experiences will only be fulfilled for the moment, and tomorrow, we will wake up with that same hunger.

Jesus told the <u>woman at the well,</u>

<u>John 4:13-14</u>
Jesus answered and said to her, *"Whoever drinks of this water will thirst again, but whoever drinks of the water that I shall give him will never thirst. But the water that I shall give him will become in him a fountain of water springing up into everlasting life."*

<u>Revelation 18:4-8</u>
"And I heard another voice from heaven saying, "Come out of her, my people, lest you share in her sins, and lest you receive of her plagues. For her sins have reached to heaven, and God has remembered her iniquities. Render to her just as she rendered to you and repay her double according to her works; in the cup which she has mixed, mix double for her. In the measure that she glorified herself and lived luxuriously, in the same measure give her torment and sorrow; for she says in her heart, 'I sit as queen, and am no widow, and will not see sorrow.' Therefore her

plagues will come in one day—death and mourning and famine. And she will be utterly burned with fire, for strong is the Lord God who judges her."

<u>**Note**</u>: While scripture refers to this religious and political system as an entity in itself, ultimately it will be the leaders and those involved with her that will experience this judgment of destruction. Politicians and greedy business empires will be held accountable and destroyed. It is interesting to see the difference in career politicians net worth when they first get into office and their net worth after several terms in office. Such a great difference.

<u>Revelation 18:9-19 Then the world will mourn Babylon's fall</u>

"The kings of the earth who committed fornication and lived luxuriously with her will weep and lament for her, when they see the smoke of her burning, standing at a distance for fear of her torment, saying, Alas, alas, that great city Babylon, that mighty city! For in one hour your judgment has come.' "And the merchants of the earth will weep and mourn over her, for no one buys their merchandise anymore: merchandise of gold and silver, precious stones and pearls, fine linen and

purple, silk and scarlet, every kind of citron wood, every kind of object of ivory, every kind of object of most precious wood, bronze, iron, and marble; and cinnamon and incense, fragrant oil and frankincense, wine and oil, fine flour and wheat, cattle and sheep, horses and chariots, and bodies and souls of men. The fruit that your soul longed for has gone from you, and all the things which are rich and splendid have gone from you, and you shall find them no more at all. The merchants of these things, who became rich by her, will stand at a distance for fear of her torment, weeping and wailing, and saying, 'Alas, alas, that great city that was clothed in fine linen, purple, and scarlet, and adorned with gold and precious stones and pearls! For in one hour such great riches came to nothing.' Every shipmaster, all who travel by ship, sailors, and as many as trade on the sea, stood at a distance and cried out when they saw the smoke of her burning, saying, What is like this great city?' They threw dust on their heads and cried out, weeping and wailing, and saying, 'Alas, alas, that great city, in which all who had ships on the sea became rich by her wealth! For in one hour she is made desolate."

Note: The destruction of this Political and Financial System and the City wherever it may be, will be destroyed quickly. It will happen much like the Wall Street crash of 1929, here in the U.S. When you take a river boat ride in San Antonio, Texas there are some buildings decorated with some gruesome Gargoyles. Our river boat guide told the story of a man who actually jumped off one of those buildings on that day when he found that he had lost all his wealth. The fact that those who did business with her cried and appeared to really care about those being destroyed. When in reality they will cry and care only because their golden goose is cooked and gone. Many career politicians and business tycoons only care about power and money. But on that day they will no longer have that power or a way of making money.

Heaven will be experiencing a celebration: Revelation 18:20-24

"Rejoice over her, O heaven, and you holy apostles and prophets, for God has avenged you on her!
Then a mighty angel took up a stone like a great millstone and threw it into the sea, saying, "Thus with violence the great city Babylon shall be thrown down, and shall not be found anymore. The sound of harpists, musicians, flutists, and trumpeters shall not be heard in you anymore. No craftsman of any craft shall be found in you anymore, and the sound of a

millstone shall not be heard in you anymore. The light of a lamp shall not shine in you anymore, and the voice of bridegroom and bride shall not be heard in you anymore. For your merchants were the great men of the earth, for by your sorcery all the nations were deceived. And in her was found the blood of prophets and saints, and of all who were slain on the earth."

Note: -Business activities and celebrations will cease. Not a sound will be heard because they will no longer exist. The tribulation believers will no longer be among them either. They will have been removed to be into God's presence. These people will weep over the destruction of Babylon but Heaven will exult and celebrate over her fall!

All of Heaven Worships
Chapter 19

Revelation 19:1
*"After these things I heard a loud voice of
a great multitude in heaven, saying, "Alleluia!
Salvation and glory and honor and power belong
to the Lord our God!"*

We have seen these words repeated many
times throughout our study, because one
Sovereign act of God leads to another. After
these things (Greek- Metah -Towtah) After
what things? Here Scripture is referring to after
all of God's judgment actions against a Christ
rejecting world have been fulfilled.

For a moment let us return to our general
outline we found in
Revelation 1:19
*"Write the things which you have seen, and
the things which are, and the things which will
take place after this."*

1. *Things which you have seen,* This would have
been the revelation of Jesus that John had on
the Island of Patmos, found in ***Rev. 1***
2. *Things which are,* This refers to **Rev. 2-3** that
speaks of the *letters Jesus wrote the 7 churches*

concerning issues that these *congregations* needed to address and correct.

3. *Things which will take place after this.* *We have looked into* **Rev. 6-18**, *verse by verse, The 7 Seals: The seven trumpets. The seven bowls we have seen all of what God's judgments on earth will be like and we are ever so grateful that we don't have to be here then.*

In **Chapters 5-6** *When John was taken into heaven to be shown the Title Deed of Earth, (scroll, the little book) and when no one is found worthy to open the 7 Seals of that book representing the beginning of the tribulation, John began to cry, until one of the elders tells him,*

Revelation 5:5

"But one of the elders said to me, "Do not weep. Behold, the Lion of the tribe of Judah, the Root of David, has prevailed to open the scroll and to loose its seven seals."

Note: Now in Chapter 19, we find this expression repeated once again, *After these things (Greek Metah -Towtah) But this time,* they mean *after* God has finished with all of His judgement on the world.

Now, John finds himself back in Heaven. He has just experienced the greatest and most terrifying *Cinematic movie humanity* will not only see, *(a Cinema not manufactured by artificial intelligence,)* these events will actually happen. People will go through so much pain and suffering through this experience. Now John must chronicle them all down for future generations to read, and so here we are! Let us now join the celebration!

V.1
Heaven celebrates!
John hears a loud voice of a great multitude in heaven, saying, "Alleluia! Salvation and glory and honor and power belong to the Lord our God!

John hears the worship in Heaven! Alleluia is a Hebrew word written in Greek, it is only found here in **Rev.19** written 4 times, but still pronounced Hallelujah.
The word hallēl in Hebrew means a "joyous praise in song." The second part, Yah, is the shortened form of YHWH. (Yahweh or Jehovah in modern English).
So it means, "joyous praise to Jehovah"

The reason this multitude is praising God, is because of God's judgments upon religious and political/economic Babylon, because they deceived so many and drew people's attention from God's truth.

Revelation 19: 2-5
"For true and righteous are His judgments, because He has judged the great harlot who corrupted the earth with her fornication; and He has avenged on her the blood of His servants shed by her." Again they said, "Alleluia! Her smoke rises up forever and ever!"

<u>Note</u>: Many years ago I preached a message urging families to purge their homes of things that shouldn't be in them. We placed everything in a 55 gallon barrel set it on fire it burned for 10-11 days. It just would not stop burning, How Revealing !

V.4-5
And the twenty-four elders and the four living creatures fell down and worshiped God who sat on the throne, saying, "<u>Amen! Alleluia!</u>" Then a voice came from the throne, saying, "Praise our God, all you His servants and those who fear Him, both small and great!"

Note:
How many times have we heard someone say, "How can a loving God bring such

destruction and send people to hell, and punish them."

The fact of the matter is that God will never send anyone to eternal punishment, or desire for them to experience tribulation. That's why He sent His son Jesus to keep people from all that. The truth is people will do that to themselves. The question is: What must a person do to go to Hell, "<u>absolutely nothing</u>." Just continue to live in sin, refuse to accept forgiveness.

So then all of God's judgments are correct.

Revelation 19:6-8
"And I heard, as it were, the voice of a great multitude, as the sound of many waters and as the sound of mighty thunderings, saying, "Alleluia! For the Lord God Omnipotent reigns! Let us be glad and rejoice and give Him glory, for the marriage of the Lamb has come, and His wife has made herself ready." And to her it was granted to be arrayed in fine linen, clean and bright, for the fine linen is the righteous acts of the saints."

Revelation 19: 9
Then he said to me, "write: Blessed are those who are called to the marriage supper of the Lamb!' " And he said to me, "These are the true sayings of God."

Note:

The Purpose of the marriage supper of the Lamb is for celebration. Jesus' bride is now united with her groom, to experience the judgment seat of Christ.

The judgment seat of Christ does not determine our salvation; that matter was settled by Christ's sacrifice on Calvary on our behalf according to

I John 2:2

"And He Himself is the propitiation for our sins, and not for ours only but also for the whole world."

Rom. 8:1

"There is therefore now no condemnation for those who are in Christ Jesus"

So, as believers we are secure in Christ, but we must still appear before the *judgment seat of Christ*. This will be a *time of examination and a time to receive our reward.* Jesus will inspect what we did with the resources we were given. How faithful were we? Did we remain yielded to the Spirit; Did we seek to honor Christ in the world? If we did, we will receive our just and due reward. But if we neglected our opportunities to serve Him. We will suffer loss of reward, but not our Salvation.

Paul compares our Christian service to erecting a building:

Each of us should build with care.
I Corinthians 3: 11-15
"For no other foundation can anyone lay than that which is laid, which is Jesus Christ. Now if anyone builds on this foundation with gold, silver, precious stones, wood, hay, straw, each one's work will become clear; for the Day will declare it, because it will be revealed by fire; and the fire will test each one's work, of what sort it is. If anyone's work which he has built on it endures, he will receive a reward. If anyone's work is burned, he will suffer loss; but he himself will be saved, yet so as through fire."

John's reaction to the Voice of the Angel
Revelation 19:10
"And I fell at his feet to worship him. But he said to me see that you do not do that! I am your fellow servant, and of your brethren who have the testimony of Jesus. Worship God! For the testimony of Jesus is the spirit of prophecy."

<u>**Note**</u>: Only God the Father and the Son are to be worshipped. There are many instances in the Bible where people worshipped Jesus, and He allowed it. He taught the people they should only worship God. Jesus allowed it, Why? Because He was letting people know <u>He is God.</u>

<u>Then John sees, Christ Coming in His 2nd Advent</u>
<u>Revelation 19: 11-16</u>

"Now I saw heaven opened, and behold, a white horse. And He who sat on him was called Faithful and True, and in righteousness He judges and makes war. His eyes were like a flame of fire, and on His head were many crowns. He had a name written that no one knew except Himself. He was clothed with a robe dipped in blood, and His name is called The Word of God. And the armies in heaven, clothed in fine linen, white and clean, followed Him on white horses. Now out of His mouth goes a Sharp Sword, that with it He should strike the nations. And He Himself will rule them with a rod of iron. He Himself treads the winepress of the fierceness and wrath of Almighty God. And He has on His robe and on His thigh a name written: KING OF KINGS AND LORD OF LORDS."

John has the privilege of prophetically seeing Jesus' return in His 2nd Advent, and the armies of Heaven behind Him ready to establish His 1000 year reign. Those armies will be none other than every born again child of God!

There will be another supper invitation.
Revelation 19: 17- 18

"Then I saw an angel standing in the sun; and he cried with a loud voice, saying to all the birds that fly in the midst of heaven, "Come and gather together for the Supper of the Great God, that you may eat the flesh of kings, the flesh of captains, the flesh of mighty men, the flesh of horses and of those who sit on them, and the flesh of all people, free and slave, both small and great."

In the future, people will have the opportunity to attend one of two banquets. The first will be the Marriage Supper of the Lamb where believers will enjoy supping with the Lord. The second invitation, will be "Dinner at Armageddon's" this is where people will become the main entry that all the birds and animals of prey will dine on after Jesus defeats them with the sword that comes forth from his mouth.

As believers we must do all we can to get as many people as possible to the Marriage Supper Of The Lamb.

<u>After the Battle of ARMAGEDDON</u>
<u>Revelation 19: 19-21</u>
"And I saw the beast, the kings of the earth, and their armies, gathered together to make war against Him who sat on the horse and against His army. Then the beast was captured, and with him the false prophet who worked signs in his presence, by which he deceived those who received the mark of the beast and those who worshiped his image. These two were cast alive into the "lake of fire" burning with brimstone. And the rest were killed with the sword which proceeded from the mouth of Him who sat on the horse, and all the birds were filled with their flesh."

Our Lord needs not to fight; but just speak the Word and His enemies are destroyed. The beast and false prophet will then be cast into the <u>Lake of Fire</u>.

In our last two chapters together we saw how God will bring total destruction to the false religious and political systems that will rule during the tribulation until they fulfill God's eternal purposes.

In this chapter we will encounter the fulfillment of what Jesus prophesied that will take place at the:

1. *"End of the tribulation,*
2. *The mil-lineal reign*
3. The *eternal state*

Let's read what Jesus said about this:
Mathew 13: 40
"Therefore as the tares are gathered and burned in the fire, so it will be at the end of this age."

In Mathew, Jesus is teaching the disciples the parable of the *Wheat and the Tares*. But He also mentions that the Dispensation of Grace will end with the Rapture, Then the Judgment and the Fiery furnace will follow.

He explains that all of these things will usher in the "*Age to Come*" – "*The Millennium*" when Satan will be bound 1,000 years.

The Millennium
Chapter 20

Revelation 20:1-3

"Then I saw an angel coming down from heaven, having the key to the bottomless pit and a great chain in his hand." He laid hold of the dragon, that serpent of old, who is the Devil and Satan, and bound him for a thousand years; and he cast him into the bottomless pit, (Abuso, means shaft) and shut him up, and set a seal on him, so that he should deceive the nations no more till the thousand years were finished. But after these things he must be released for a little while."

Note : *Again we* find the same words a*fter these things*: *(Greek translation, Metah - Towtah)* transitioning us from one event to another.

Revelation 20: 2

"He laid hold of the dragon, that serpent of old, who is the Devil and Satan, and bound him for a thousand years;"

This passage leaves no question as to who this is, the Devil himself. He will be thrown into the Abuso - the depthless pit, a shaft or an Abyss. This Abuso appears to be a holding place where fallen angelic beings and evil spirits are sent to be incarcerated. It is the place that will house Satan for 1,000 years.

In the book of **_Luke 8_**, When Jesus was casting out the demons out of the Gadarene man, the legion of spirits in him begged Jesus.

Luke 8:31
"And they begged Him that He would not command them to go out into the <u>abyss</u>."

Also in **_Revelation 9,_** at the time of the 5th trumpet angel a Star was given the key to this Abuso. When he opened it, out of the smoke crawled locusts with the venom of scorpions. So satan will be held in this Abyss during the Millennium.

The saints will reign with Christ 1,000 Years
Revelation 20: 4
"And I saw thrones, and they sat on them, and judgment was committed to them. Then I saw the souls of those who had been beheaded for their witness to Jesus and for the word of God, who had not worshiped the beast or his image, and had not received his mark on their foreheads or on their hands. And they lived and reigned with Christ for a thousand years."

__Note__: This scripture is often misunderstood, by individuals who believe in a __Post Tribulation Rapture Theology.__ That believers will have to go thru and experience the __Wrath of God__ in the tribulation. This happens because the passage is being misinterpreted as if though John was speaking of __only one Group of people.__ Let's read and understand it the way it is written and meant to be understood.

__1st Group__
"And I saw thrones, and __they__ sat on them, and __judgment was committed to them.__"

This is the __first Group__, this is the Church. These are the blessed of the __Resurrection__, at the coming of our Lord.
Not only will they receive rewards at the marriage supper of the Lamb, but they will also be given the right to reign and rule with Him.

__2nd Group__
"Then I saw the souls of those who had been beheaded for their witness to Jesus and for the word of God, who had not worshiped the beast or his image, and had not received his mark on their foreheads or on their hands. And they lived and reigned with Christ for a thousand years."

This is clearly another group of believers; they are the tribulations saints, who will refuse to take the mark of the beast, or to worship his image.

Both Groups shall become priests of God and of Christ, and shall reign with Him a thousand years, along with the Old Testament saints according to ***Dan. 12:2.***

Both groups will be given an opportunity to reign, rule and judge with our Lord.

These are things that will happen then!
1. Jesus will return to take Possession of Earth, along with those He redeemed on the Cross and resurrected will return with Him.
2. We will reign alongside of Him.
3. Satan will be cast into the Abuso.
4. The earth will experience a level of restoration. Some theologians believe that earth will return to its original state as it was before the fall. So the earth will be a Paradise.
5. There will be true climate change!
6. There will be a new longevity of life (for the mortal).
7. The Earth will be beautiful and filled with His righteousness as waters cover the Sea.

Fulfilling the prophesy of:
Habakkuk 2:14

"For the earth will be filled with the knowledge of the glory of the LORD, as the waters cover the sea."

Jesus' first order of business will be to gather those who survived the tribulation and see who will be allowed to enter the kingdom age. Those who took the mark will not be allowed to enter. If they worshipped the beast they will not be allowed in. It is then that the statement Jesus made in **Matthew 25** will come into play. It will be in this moment when the Lord will separate His people the sheep from the goats, like the shepherd does.

Matthew 25: 32-36

"All the nations will be gathered before Him, and He will separate them one from another, as a shepherd divides his sheep from the goats. And He will set the sheep on His right hand, but the goats on the left. Then the King will say to those on His right hand, 'Come, you blessed of My Father, inherit the kingdom prepared for you from the foundation of the world: for I was hungry and you gave Me food; I was thirsty and you gave Me drink; I was a stranger and you took Me in; I was naked and you clothed Me; I

was sick and you visited Me; I was in prison and you came to Me"

This group will be from those who will have survived the tribulation. After the 1,000 years there will be another resurrection to take place! Those who did not receive Jesus as Lord.

Revelation 20: 5-6
"But the rest of the dead did not live again until the thousand years were finished this is the first resurrection."

<u>Note</u>: Those who rejected Jesus will not be resurrected until 1,000 years later, after the Millennium. These are the people who will stand before the great White Throne Judgment!

Revelation 20:6
"Blessed and holy is he who has part in the first resurrection. Over such the second death has no power, but they shall be priests of God and of Christ, and shall reign with Him a thousand years."

Then Satan will be loosed for a small season!

Revelation 20: 7-10

"*Now when the thousand years have expired, Satan will be released from his prison and will go out to deceive the nations which are in the four corners of the earth, Gog and Magog, to gather them together to battle, whose number is as the sand of the sea. They went up on the breadth of the earth and surrounded the camp of the saints and the beloved city. And fire came down from God out of heaven and devoured them. The devil, who deceived them, was cast into the lake of fire and brimstone where the beast and the false prophet are. And they will be tormented day and night forever and ever*"

When I first read this passage, I asked the question, WHY? If Satan caused so much pain and suffering, Why would God want to turn him loose again? The answer is simple when you take the time to think things through. As with all of God's creation, Satan serves God's divine purposes.

The Millennium will be an interim period of time between the battle of Armageddon and the battle of Gog and Magog. This will be the last battle. Jesus will crush this satanic rebellion once and for all!

**Ezekiel 38-39** The _Prophet Ezekiel gives a detailed description of this last battle and the end results._

Who are these nations? In Biblical history, Magog was Noah's grandson. (_**Gen. 10:2**_) His descendants settled in Europe, north of Israel.

Ezekiel tells this story. The indication is that Russia will be the Magog of scripture. Ezekiel prophesies about this Battle,

**Ezekiel 38: 8-9**
"In the latter years you will come into the land of those brought back from the sword and gathered from many people on the mountains of Israel, which had long been desolate; they were brought out of the nations, and now all of them dwell safely. You will ascend, coming like a storm, covering the land like a cloud, you and all your troops and many peoples with you."

**Ezekiel 38:10**
"'Thus says the Lord GOD: "On that day it shall come to pass that thoughts will arise in your mind, and you will make an evil plan"

Ezekiel 38:15
"Then you will come from your place out of the far north, you and many people's with you, all of them riding on horses, a great company and a mighty army."

Ezekiel 38:22
"And I will bring him to judgment with pestilence and bloodshed; I will rain down on him, on his troops, and on the many peoples who are with him, flooding rain, great hailstones, fire, and brimstone."

Ezekiel 39:7-8
"So I will make My holy name known in the midst of My people Israel, and I will not let them profane My holy name anymore. Then the nations shall know that I am the LORD, the Holy One in Israel. Surely it is coming, and it shall be done," says the Lord GOD. "This is the day of which I have spoken."

Coming back to the thought that satan serves God's eternal purposes. When we are first born again, we begin with such great zeal and passion. So that we make commitments like "I love you Lord and want to live my life for you, but as we continue on our Life's Journey we find that saying and doing are two very different things. I can easily say "I love you Lord, but find it's not as easy to live it out.

I will use an Illustration, I heard Chuck Smith say if your father asked you to stay and help him on a project, but had to tie you down to make sure you stayed until he returned. Upon his return if you were still there, would that be an expression of your love, obedience, and devotion to him, NO!

If you remained faithful without being secured, this did not matter. Regardless of how long it took for him to return even if others (satan) came to invite you somewhere else but you remained, then that would be an expression of your love. That's what God expects from us, He doesn't want to tie us down and obligate us to love Him. He wants us to remain freely and willingly committed until He returns. So to say, I love you Lord and really not mean it, can happen to us all! Satan is often the instrument that God uses for us to see or to measure our true level of love and commitment for Him. God already knows how much we really do or don't mean what we say. But it is for us to see where we measure up to our commitment.

There's another reason satan will play out that role. There will be many to be born during Jesus' 1,000 year reign and they must deal with their own freewill decision. Will they receive salvation or follow sin? We can see this principle lived out in Job's life. When God pointed Job out to satan to see how much Job loved him, satan answered, anyone would love you if you blessed them like you have Job. You have even placed a hedge of protection about him. Take the hedge off and let me at him and you will see how much he doesn't love you. So God allowed satan to touch Job!

Take a moment and ask yourself, "Am I only serving God for the blessings? For the benefits or am I serving God, because I truly love him with all my heart."

God-allowed Job to be stripped of all he owned. He lost it all, family, funds, and friends.

Job 1:21
"Naked I came from my mother's womb, naked I'll return to the womb of the earth.
GOD gives, GOD takes. God's name be ever blessed."

Satan's thoughts of Job were that the only reason he served God were for the blessings, but he found out, that was not so, <u>Job really loved God!</u>

<u>The Great White Throne Judgment</u>

<u>Revelation 20: 11-15</u>
"Then I saw a <u>great white throne</u> and Him who sat on it, from whose face the earth and the heaven fled away. And there was found no place for them. And I saw the dead, small and great, standing before God, and books were opened. And another book was opened, which is the <u>Book of Life.</u> And the dead were judged according to their works, by the things which were written in the books. The sea gave up the dead who were in it, and Death and Hades delivered up the dead who were in them. And they were judged, each one according to his works. Then Death and Hades were cast into the <u>lake of fire.</u> This is the second death. And anyone not found written in the Book of Life was cast into the lake of fire."

<u>Listen to the words Jesus will Say,</u> <u>Matthew 7:21-23</u>
"Not everyone who says to Me, Lord, Lord,' shall enter the kingdom of heaven, but he who does the will of My Father in heaven. Many will say to

Me in that day, 'Lord, Lord, have we not prophesied in Your name, cast out demons in Your name, and done many wonders in Your name?' And then I will declare to them, 'I never knew you; depart from Me, you who practice lawlessness!'

Note:
<u>The Lake of Fire:</u> This *final destination* was designed for satan, the beast and the false prophet.

Description of the White Throne Judgment!

In <u>**Revelation 4,**</u> John saw God's Throne. In all of its Greatness. The Greatness mentioned here is because of the magnitude of the occasion "<u>*Judgment Time*</u>" is about to come forth from it. "So great is this moment, that the *Heavens and earth will run away* from the presence of Him who sits on the throne. This is the final judgment before the new heavens and the new earth are brought into being.

Revelations 21; *All things are made new.*
In the next two chapters, John begins to describe the New Jerusalem, the City of God. Where the bride of Christ will live with Him.

The New Heaven and New Earth
Chapter 21

Revelation 21:1
"Now I saw a new heaven and a new earth, for the first heaven and the first earth had passed away. Also there was no more sea."

Psalm 102: coincides with this verse, it speaks of God's Handiwork and God's unchanging Nature.

Vs. 25-27
"Of old You laid the foundation of the earth, and the heavens are the work of Your hands. They will perish, but You will endure; Yes, they will all grow old like a garment; Like a cloak You will change them, and they will be changed. But You are the same, and Your years will have no end."

The prophet Isaiah records of God,
Isaiah 65: 17-19
"For behold, I create new heavens and a new earth; and the former shall not be remembered or come to mind. But be glad and rejoice forever in what I create;
For behold, I create Jerusalem as a rejoicing, and her people a joy. I will rejoice in Jerusalem, and joy in My people; the voice of weeping shall no longer be heard in her, nor the voice of crying"

The word create here is the Hebrew word "Bara."
The same word used in **Genesis 1:1**. *When God*
created the world originally. It means to bring
something out of nothing "Ex- Nihillo" (Latin)

But there is also another word used in Genesis
for create and that is "Asah" which means
to reform or rebuild from what already exists.
Asah, is the word God uses in the rest of Genesis
to explain what He did to restore our present
earth for us to live in. This further establishes a
foundation for the Gap Theory of time, believed
to have existed between
Gen. 1:1 and Gen. 1:2 *These verses further*
reinforce God's promise of a new Heaven and
Earth.

Isaiah 66:22
"For as the new heavens and the new earth
which I will make shall remain before Me," says
the LORD, "So shall your descendants and your
name remain."

Matthew 24:35
"Heaven and earth will pass away, but My words
will by no means pass away."

Peter explains how these New Heavens and
Earth will happen!

2 Peter 3:10-13

"But the <u>Day of the Lord</u> will come as a thief in the night, in which the heavens will pass away with a great noise, and the elements will melt with fervent heat; both the earth and the works that are in it will be burned up. Therefore, since all these things will be dissolved, what manner of persons ought you to be in holy conduct and godliness, looking for and hastening the coming of the day of God, because of which the heavens will be dissolved, being on fire, and the elements will melt with fervent heat? Nevertheless we, according to His promise, look for new heavens and a new earth in which righteousness dwells."

Each of these Prophetic scriptures speak of a new Heaven and a new Earth that God will Create "<u>Bara.</u>"
But even with all these facts, some still say that Earth as we know it, is eternal and will remain the same. Not So!

Scientific studies teach us about atomic energy. They say that atoms are made up of protons, neutrons, and electrons. Negatively charged electrons revolve around the protons and neutrons of an atom. Protons are positively charged and like everything else in life that are alike.

They have a tendency to push against/away from each other. Much like the two matching poles of a magnet.

Let me give you a human example (You) as an atom. Why is it that the people you find more fault in, dislike the most, criticize, and at times push away from are oftentimes the ones that are the most like you? So the question is, What is it that holds these protons together? They should by nature tear apart. Yet they are held together by the strongest power known to man, a fundamental force. Science has no other name for it other than to call it the "Strong Force." Scientists only have a name for it but no explanation. They just don't fully understand it. What else could this Strong Force be, other than the Hand of the Power of God? We have all seen the destructive power of the atomic bomb in Japan. It is said the power that holds atoms together is even stronger than that.

Isaiah 40:12
"Who has measured the waters in the hollow of His hand, Measured heaven with a span
And calculated the dust of the earth in a measure? Weighed the mountains in scales
And the hills in a balance?"

Psalm 24:1-2

"The earth is the LORD's, and all its fullness, the world and those who dwell therein.
For He has founded it upon the seas, and established it upon the waters."

Revelation 21: 2-4

"Then I, John, saw the holy city, New Jerusalem, coming down out of heaven from God, prepared as a bride adorned for her husband. And I heard a loud voice from heaven saying, "Behold, the tabernacle of God is with men, and He will dwell with them, and they shall be His people. God Himself will be with them and be their God. And God will wipe away every tear from their eyes; there shall be no more death, nor sorrow, nor crying. There shall be no more pain, for the former things have passed away."

<u>**Note**</u>: For generations Christians have been taught that believers will all go to heaven and live there for eternity. But that's not what scripture teaches! This passage says the Heaven will come down to Earth. God himself will come to live with us!

Revelation 21: 5-8

Then He who sat on the throne said, "Behold, I make all things new." And He said to me, "Write, for these words are true and faithful. And He said to me, "It is done! I am the Alpha and the Omega, the Beginning and the End. I will give of the fountain of the water of life freely to him who thirsts. He who overcomes shall inherit all things, and I will be his God and he shall be My son. But the cowardly, unbelieving, abominable, murderers, sexually immoral, sorcerers, idolaters, and all liars shall have their part in the lake which burns with fire and brimstone, which is the second death."

The word translated "cowardly" in this passage refers to fearfulness and timidity. In today's terms a *coward* is someone who lacks the courage to do difficult, dangerous, or unpleasant things. They consciously shy away from unpleasant situations, doing whatever they can to save their own skin, making themselves slaves to fear. *The Bible has much to say about being a slave to fear and contains stories of some godly people who gave in to fear."*

2 Timothy 1:7
"*For God has not given us a spirit of fear, but of power and of love and of a sound mind.*"

Revelation 21: 9-13 *The New Jerusalem*
(Ezekiel 48:30–35)

"*Then one of the seven Angels who had the seven bowls filled with the seven last plagues came to me and talked with me, saying, "Come, I will show you the bride, the Lamb's wife." And he carried me away in the Spirit to a great and high mountain, and showed me the great city, the holy Jerusalem, descending out of heaven from God, having the glory of God. Her light was like a most precious stone, like a jasper stone, clear as crystal. Also she had a great and high wall with twelve gates, and twelve angels at the gates, and names written on them, which are the names of the twelve tribes of the children of Israel: three gates on the east, three gates on the north, three gates on the south, and three gates on the west.*"

<u>**Note:**</u> The New Jerusalem will be a beautiful place. John saw it as "a bride adorned for her husband" A bride prepares meticulously to look her best for her wedding day, so this implies that God plans to present the New Jerusalem as an exceptionally beautiful carefully arranged city.

Revelation 21: 14-21

"Now the wall of the city had twelve foundations, and on them were the names of the twelve apostles of the Lamb. And he who talked with me had a gold reed to measure the city, its gates, and its wall. The City is laid out as a square; its length is as great as its breadth. And he measured the city with the reed: twelve thousand furlongs. Its length, breadth, and height are equal. Then he measured its wall: one hundred and forty-four cubits, according to the measure of a man, that is, of an angel. The construction of its wall was of jasper; and the city was pure gold, like clear glass. The foundations of the wall of the city were adorned with all kinds of precious stones: the first foundation was jasper, the second sapphire, the third chalcedony, the fourth emerald, the fifth sardonyx, the sixth sardius, the seventh chrysolite, the eighth beryl, the ninth topaz, the tenth chrysoprase, the eleventh jacinth, and the twelfth amethyst. The twelve gates were twelve pearls: each individual gate was of one pearl. And the street of the city was pure gold, like transparent glass."

As I previously explained; a <u>Span</u> is a measurement from the tip of your thumb to the tip of your little finger, usually about 6 inches. <u>Cubit</u>- is a measurement from the tip of your middle finger to your elbow, about 18 inches. _Reed_-Measures 6 cubits or about 9 feet. Now we have a _Furlong_- It is 1/8 of a mile, approx. 660 ft.

The New Jerusalem will be 1400 miles wide, 1400 miles long, 1400 miles high. With 12 foundations or levels Just imagine how many people will be able to abide there. That's just the city, we will have access to the entire world.

Revelation 21: 22-27 **The Glory of the New Jerusalem**

"But I saw no temple in it, for the Lord God Almighty and the Lamb are its temple. The city had no need of the sun or of the moon to shine in it, for the glory of God illuminated it. The Lamb is its light. And the nations of those who are saved shall walk in its light, and the kings of the earth bring their glory and honor into it. Its gates shall not be shut at all by day (there shall be no night there). And they shall bring the glory and the honor of the nations into it. But there shall by no means enter it anything that defiles, or causes an abomination or a lie, but only those who are written in the Lamb's Book of Life."

There will be no need of a temple or source of light. There will be no night, there will be nothing that defiles.

Only those whose names are written in the Lambs Book of Life. We will forever experience the fulfillment of God's eternal plans He intended for man to enjoy when He created him. God gives John the privilege of a glimpse of a world without war and evil, only happiness and fellowship among the nations.

Revelations 22: 1-5 John *now continues to describe the New Jerusalem.* It is the City of God, the city that the Old Testament saints were looking for the river of life.

"And he (Same Angel) showed me a pure river of water of life, clear as crystal, proceeding from the throne of God and of the Lamb. In the river, middle of its street, and on either side of the river, was the tree of life, which bore twelve fruits, each tree yielding its fruit every month. The leaves of the tree were for the healing of the nations. And there shall be no more curse, but the throne of God and of the Lamb shall be in it, and His servants shall serve Him. They shall see His face, and His name shall be on their foreheads. There shall be no night there: They need no lamp nor light of the

sun, for the Lord God gives them light. And they shall reign forever and ever."

<u>Ezekiel</u> mentions these same healing waters and a tree.
<u>Ezekiel 47:1</u>
"Then he brought me back to the door of the temple; and there was water, flowing from under the threshold of the temple toward the east, for the front of the temple faced east; the water was flowing from under the right side of the temple, south of the altar."

When God created the Garden of Eden, He placed a t<u>ree of life.</u> Here we see the re-appearance of that tree once again, along with a river of life. The purpose for the River of life and the tree of life will be for the <u>healing of the nations.</u>

Even-though Adam failed, God's redeemed people will be restored to a greater environment where God not only walks and communes with us, but He will dwell with us also and meet our every need.

It is peculiar that of all the trees available to him, Adam chose to eat of the tree of death and not the tree of life. But before we judge him for his decision, think about it, isn't that what people do today. They continue to eat of the tree of death and not go to the tree of life called Calvary.

Revelation 22: 6-11 *The Time Is Near*
"Then he said to me, "These words are faithful and true." And the Lord God of the holy prophets sent His angel to show His servants the things which must shortly take place. "Behold, I am coming quickly! Blessed is he who keeps the words of the prophecy of this book." Now I, John, saw and heard these things. And when I heard and saw, I fell down to worship before the feet of the angel who showed me these things. Then he said to me, "See that you do not do that for I am your fellow servant, and of your brethren the prophets and of those who keep the words of this book. Worship God." And he said to me, "Do not seal the words of the prophecy of this book, for the time is at hand. He who is unjust, let him be unjust still; he who is filthy, let him be filthy still; he who is righteous, let him be righteous still; he who is holy, let him be holy still."

<u>**Note:**</u> Jesus Promises to come quickly. He did not mean in the next few moments, but when He does come it will be quick. Yet in our time it's been 2,000 years. But, we must remember that God lives in eternity. He is ever present in

all of life's yesterdays, today, and all our tomorrows. He has no time constraints!

We must take note that in the Book of Daniel. God told him to seal the book until the Time of the End. (**_Dan. 12:4_**) but to John he says *"Don't Seal them"* for the time is at hand!

Then John wanted to bow down and Worship this Angel. But He is forbidden. The Angel told him "For I am your fellow servant,"

2 Peter 3: 3-9
"knowing this first: that scoffers will come in the last days, walking according to their own lusts, and saying, "Where is the promise of His coming? For since the fathers fell asleep, all things continue as they were from the beginning of creation." For this they willfully forget: that by the word of God the heavens were of old, and the earth standing out of water and in the water, by which the world that then existed perished, being flooded with water. But the heavens and the earth which are now preserved by the same word, are reserved for fire until the day of judgment and perdition of ungodly men. But, beloved, do not forget this one thing, that with the Lord one day is as a thousand years, and a thousand years as one day. The Lord is not slack concerning His promise, as some

count slackness, but is longsuffering toward us, not willing that any should perish but that all should come to repentance."

So for God, it's just been two days. He is waiting for the Church to "Cast the net of His Love" Into the sea of broken humanity and rescue those willing to receive Jesus as Lord!

__Revelation 22:12-21__ *Jesus testifies to the churches*
"And behold, I am coming quickly, and My reward is with Me, to give to everyone according to his work. I am the Alpha and the Omega, the beginning and the end, the first and the last."- Blessed are those who do His commandments that they may have the right to the tree of life and may enter through the gates into the city. But outside are dogs and sorcerers and sexually immoral and murderers and idolaters, and whoever loves and practices a lie. "I, Jesus, have sent My angel to testify to you these things in the churches. I am the Root and the Offspring of David, the Bright and Morning Star." And the Spirit and the bride say, "Come!" And let him who hears say, "Come!" And let him who thirsts come. Whoever desires let him take the water of life freely.

A Warning!

"For I testify to everyone who hears the words of the prophecy of this book: If anyone adds to these things, God will add to him the plagues that are written in this book; and if anyone takes away from the words of the book of this prophecy, God shall take away his part from the Book of Life, from the holy city, and from the things which are written in this book.

He who testifies to these things says,

Surely I Am Coming Quickly

Amen. Even so, come, Lord Jesus!

The grace of our Lord Jesus Christ be with you all. Amen."

Prayer,

Lord, now that we better understand the Book of Revelation, our prayer is that you use each of us as instruments of direction, light, help, hope, and healing. We understand you will hold each of us responsible for this deposit of your word. Let what we have read ignite each of us to action. Let us not be hearers only but doers of your word. For we know that we will stand before you one day to give an account for our actions and how we spent this Currency of Time you have given each of us..

Let us be found Faithful! Amen

Bibliography
Casting Crowns – Slow Fade
Chuck Smith Commentary
Dake's Annotated Bible
Dake's – God's Plan for Man
Foxe' Book of Martyrs
Got Questions.com
Halley's Bible Handbook
Open Doors International: Opendoors.org
Provision of History (Dr. Elizabeth Williams)
Revelation (Dr. Bill Creasy on Audible)
Strong's Concordance
Strong's Exhaustive Dictionary
Vines Expository Bible
Wayne Jackson (From The Chrisitan Courier)